AF378960

4 Simple Rules of Personal Finance

Wise Up to Rise Up

By Sue Sorensen

For permission requests, write to the publisher,
"Attention: Permissions Coordinator."

What Really Matters® Publishing
827 N Hollywood Way #522
Burbank, CA 91505
www.wrmpublishing.com
mail@wrmpublishing.com

ISBN: 978 1 7359157 0 8   Paperback Print Edition
ISBN: 978 1 7359157 1 5   E-Book Edition

Introduction

Maybe it's time for you to wise up financially. For me, learning about and improving my financial situation began many years ago, when I was in my twenties, working two jobs, dead broke, and deeply in debt.

I was raised in a *lower* economic class home on the east side of Los Angeles. My mother had four kids and was absent from our home weekdays from early morning to evening. She was a secretary in downtown L.A. and certainly did not make much money, but her income was steady. My father, on the other hand, was rarely employed, and later abandoned the family altogether. We were four typical latch-key kids. We wore second-hand or homemade clothes. I have a favorite picture of my mother and the four of us kids, and in it my sister and I are both barefoot: me with dirty, patched-knee pants; my sister in clothes that are visibly too small; my brother in pants that had holes in the knees. That picture, which you can see in the last pages of this book, really tells the story of my early life. For most of my childhood my family lived in an older, rented house, where the roof leaked in the rain, and where it was not unusual for the telephone or electricity to be turned off briefly for non-payment. When I read *The Hillbilly Elegy* by J.D. Vance last year I related to many aspects of his story; I felt that I had lived a similar, city version of his dysfunctional upbringing.

I do not share this because I am looking for sympathy. In fact, I believe that my family and our circumstances were not lamentable. Not advantaged, but not so bad. We were not abused. We didn't go hungry. I understand that many other people come from much more challenging or desperate upbringings. My point is that I, like *many* people in the world, did not come from a financially secure home. When you are raised in a financially sketchy environment, the lessons you learn about money, work, or finances may be skewed from the types of lessons learned in more financially secure homes. Wealthy homes provide altogether different lessons, I'm sure.

Much of what I learned about money and finances as a child, I learned covertly and without explanation. I seemed to just know not to ask for a longed-for toy at Christmas because it was too expensive. I instinctively felt discomfort when we entered a store with products that were clearly beyond our family's means. I noted the snobbish or suspicious eyeing of my clothes, and the snubbing of the kids in my family from the more affluent kids' social activities. I certainly felt the economic alienation. In response, by my teens I was exhibiting self-defeating distain for the "haves" of the world.

Still, I was never told by my mother or by the world at large that a person's financial situation was subject to choice or to change. Of course, I wished that our family had more money. My desire for more money, though, was more of a fantasy or a daydream than a goal. I had no idea and was never instructed about there being actual actions I might take to achieve financial goals. Instead I did whatever I could do to get money, babysitting or cleaning people's houses in my early teens, and taking any job I could get later.

When I entered adulthood, moving out from my mother's care at sixteen, my personal income remained very low. I was able to go to college on a scholarship, and during those years I worked as a waitress part-time. While in college I lived in circumstances which can only be referred to as marginal. For a time, I and several other shiftless kids lived in a two-room back house—if you can call it that—with a toilet but no shower and no kitchen. Another period of my late teens was spent living in a fifteen-foot travel trailer. The trailer had no bathroom at all, but it was parked in a trailer park with a nearby communal bathroom and shower. I understand, as someone who has lived very close to the financial precipice, how easily one can become ensconced in what I call "living low." I still know people from that time who never left this lifestyle of living off-the-grid, or on the dole, or off of others, or otherwise just eking out a hand-to-mouth existence.

Back then I too was certainly living hand-to-mouth, but I stayed in school and kept a job. College had been a surprise gift for me, based on good grades and poverty, but I had no guidance in college selection or curriculum. So, though I did graduate from college, I had a bachelor's degree in the rosy career major of Anthropology. I have never worked a day in any job related to that degree. After graduating I continued to live a marginal life, accepting day jobs that paid very little, so little that I often worked a second job as a waitress in the evening. I was on a path towards a lifetime of living low.

It was while I was in my mid-twenties that someone at my day job, hearing my sad-sack, no-money refrain, suggested that I might want to educate myself about money and careers. She suggested the book *Think and Grow Rich*, by Napoleon Hill. "You are the master of your destiny. You can influence, direct and control your own environment. You can make your life what you want it to be." It was good advice, and a powerful message for me back then that still holds up today. That book was a starting place for eventually taking control of and responsibility for my financial circumstances. At the time, I was working as an administrative assistant at a film studio. I worked full time and my income was in the $20,000 range. Still, that amount was twice what I had been making for the many years I had been working before. It was a humble starting place for taking control of my financial life.

Think and Grow Rich and countless other such books I've read since that time have helped me, guided my personal financial decisions, and contributed to my current financial well-being. Still, no book I ever read on finances addressed some of the root causes of *my* financial struggles or those prevalent among my acquaintances and, I suspect, those of a large percentage of the American population. Books on finances typically focus on people of "a certain level"—people who come from nice families with good careers and steady incomes. People who might easily adopt financial principles presented in some book. But that world is not the world we all come from, certainly not the world I came from. So, in synthesizing the many lessons of personal finance that I have learned—sometimes slowly and sometimes painfully—*I will* start at the beginning with a first, basic rule, and with no assumptions.

This first rule is: work. In this book I do not assume that work or successful career management is a given in understanding and managing one's personal finances. Nor do I assume that all work provides a comfortable income. Nor that any person can or should aspire to some form of work that will lead to millions of dollars in income. The first rule of personal finances is to simply to work and I will explore the topics of work and of the second rule, managing your finances, from various perspectives including, occasionally, a sociological one. I will also consider how differing individual viewpoints about work and money can and do impact an individual's financial outcomes. I will even touch on dating and parenting.

Finally, I include some basic education about pay structures, navigating a career, and creating a budget. I include these because *I* was not particularly knowledgeable about career management or about managing finances, even for many of the years I was a working adult. In the remaining chapters we will explore the two other rules, which are more traditionally associated with personal finances, that is, saving and investing.

I consider my late twenties a turning point in my adulthood. As I mentioned, I began reading books on personal finances, career management, and wealth-building. I became committed to "wising up" so to speak. Having come from a home and upbringing that offered little instruction on career or money management, I seemed to continually be struggling financially. I frequently bounced checks, had exactly zero savings, and regularly juggled my considerable debt from card to card despite working full time and sometimes working a second job. And on top of all this I was living in a tiny one bedroom flat and driving a beat-up old car.

Once committed, I studied those books and attempted to apply the knowledge I gained. I went back to school, twice, and though I always did well in school I struggled to find a clear direction educationally, and more importantly to find a clear path in my work life. Still, over the years, with some false starts and with slow, painful improvements, I can say I *have* achieved some success. In fact, I am now quite comfortable financially, a status I long felt was unattainable. Watching others struggle, particularly young people in my sphere, in recent years I've offered or been asked to coach family and friends on some of the key concepts I've learned.

Recently, however, when I was presenting some of this sage advice, my targeted pupil pointed out that, given my current income and financial situation, perhaps any advice I had to offer was unrealistic when compared to his own modest situation. He said that from my lofty, successful perspective perhaps I might not be providing pertinent advice to someone just starting out or to someone experiencing a financial crisis.

I argued the point, mentioning that I had certainly started from very humble beginnings, have had at least two significant financial slumps, and took many years to get to my current financial position. This argument served as a catalyst for this book. I *have* been relatively successful in the later years of my adulthood, based on some simple principles that I adopted, but mind you, I am not rich.

Though I have a comfortable financial portfolio and good prospects for my upcoming retirement, the real point is that my advice is geared toward helping people get to this level, a level where they might feel similarly comfortable. I do not make or have millions of dollars, and if you are looking for a book about making millions of dollars, well, this might not be the book for you. But I do have financial security, and that is the focus of this book.

When it comes to personal finances, our society imposes a veil of secrecy around money and money management. We are taught that any specific sharing about our financial situation is in bad taste. I was told when writing this book that I shared too many of my financial specifics. This secrecy works against poor and modest-income people. I'm not suggesting that you tell everyone what you make, or discuss how much you are saving, or discuss your debt and income ratios. But not sharing information makes it harder to know what is good or not good, financially speaking. I suffered for years, quietly bouncing checks and juggling my credit debt, while making extremely low wages. But this struggle seemed normal to me, because I came from a financially struggling family. At times I suspected I was managing my finances poorly. Certainly, I was not doing as well as I wanted to be doing. But I but did not have specific, comparative data to use to assess my situation.

This ignorance—yes, ignorance—perpetuates the financial problems of lower-income people. Here's an example. In my first exempt corporate job, that is, a job that paid an annual salary, not an hourly wage, I was asked about my salary/income history. After I answered I was offered and accepted a salary amount just above my most recent, quite low, annual income. Later I found out that I was *by far* the lowest paid "specialist" in the company. In fact, I was paid so much lower than others that after a few months my boss requested a substantial "equity adjustment" for me, as he put it, just to get me in the ballpark of what others were being paid.

Not knowing about pay scales can hurt you. New laws are in place forbidding prospective employers from inquiring about and basing pay on the candidate's prior work history to try to avoid underpaying the historically underpaid. But this is just one example of how being uninformed can translate into perpetuation of financial woes for those who have not been educated about personal finances. I did not know I was accepting a very low, subnormal wage.

Another example is when setting a "savings" goal amount for my retirement in a self-study course on success, I listed $50,000 as my "stretch goal" for savings. That is nowhere near enough of a retirement savings goal, but how would I know that? Learning about finances is the answer.

The system *is* rigged against you. The sad truth is that the best resources and tools are offered to rich or well-to-do people. I enrolled in a certification program in financial planning to expand my knowledge and credibility while writing this book. The program focused about 75% of its content on working with clients with significant financial resources. The rest was just concepts and law. It had whole courses on tax planning, estate planning, and guiding investments. No part of the curriculum dealt with lower-income situations.

I understand. Financial planners want to earn money, and most are employed by industries that make their money from helping people who have money make more money. I honestly hope that those topics will be pertinent for some of my readers as you improve and control your personal finances. Those topics are not the focus of this book, however. Based on my personal experience and perspective, this book focuses on the those of us who also need, perhaps more pressingly need, help understanding the basics of financial management.

This book accepts any possible starting place and does not judge you for beginning with little financial sophistication. What the book cannot provide is the desire and willingness to make changes in your life. If you sincerely want to rise up and be more financially successful, you have to choose to wise up. *Four Simple Rules* is a primer—a book certainly helpful for those that come from humble or disadvantaged homes. I also think that this book can be beneficial for the many average workers who might be struggling with or somewhat askew in their financial and career lives. Sure, the rich and some savvy others may know most of the content and intuitively abide by the rules, but many of the rest of us can use the lessons.

Rule One: Work

Why don't you get a damn job!
-My mom talking to my dad

Your career is the engine of your wealth.
-Paul Clitheroe

Understanding Differing Work Ethics

Understanding finances and the relationship of personal finances to one's work and life is quite complex. Not every person is wired to think or feel about money, work, or lifestyle the same way. A surprising fact is that there are people who do not particularly care to exert themselves for money or to amass wealth. For highly motivated people, this can be hard to understand. Representatives on both sides of the political spectrum may be baffled by the financially indifferent. The capitalist-minded right might wonder why folks living on the margins don't simply take advantage of the freedom in our country to improve their finances and lives. The socially compassionate left might not quite understand why pressing such people toward improved circumstances with assistance and handouts may ultimately do little to change their place in society.

My own father was disinclined to work much and was not unhappy. My mother's salary was low but apparently sufficient for his needs. Her income provided my father with food, gas money, cigarettes, and a roof over his head. Obviously, as a family with four kids, we could have used an income from my father, but he just didn't care much about working.

The fact is that some people are satisfied earning meager sums of money for doing some minimal version of work, or not working at all and surviving through the care and consideration of others. Satisfied is probably not the perfect word, since I believe those people might say they are not satisfied, and yet their continuing or habitual behavior tells its own story. In some cases, their very limited income might come from passive systems such as disability or welfare, or they might work part-time, get paid under the table, have intermittent jobs, or in extreme cases could even simply be panhandling or collecting recyclables. This considerable population of marginal income Americans live on the outer peripheries of what average people today might consider an adequate lifestyle, or, like my father, on the coattails of the productivity of others.

As uncomfortable as this opinion is, I have no problem with people choosing to live on the financial edges. I, myself, lived on the edges for years. If a person is taking care of their basic needs, if they are not violent or criminal, then I try hard not to judge. I don't even begrudge my father his unemployment. My father's lack of income because of his resistance to gainful employment was much more my mother's problem than mine. She was married to him and had to suffer over the bills; *she* had to make excuses for her feckless spouse; *she* suffered. As a young kid I was not tuned into my father's insolvency, other than clearly understanding that we did not have much money. My father's role in that predicament was vague to me as a child, at least until years later.

Still, though never financially successful, my father was not a bad person. He was smart, funny and a good athlete. He just rarely worked. I don't believe we, as a society, can reasonably say that all the people with minimal incomes must work harder, work more, or strive to change their lives to make more money or otherwise achieve a higher living standard. Some people simply will not. Nor do I feel that society is obliged to provide the marginal income folks with a higher living standard. I am not so socialistic as to believe that our society must provide all people with an arbitrarily defined income or associated lifestyle. I spent many of my years living low, on the edge of poverty, and felt no particular need for the intervention of others on my behalf.

I do believe that those who are willing to work full-time should be entitled to a reasonable minimum wage. That standard or minimum should provide a worker with basic subsistence, the ability to pay modest rent, have modest amenities, and eat modestly. Beyond this minimum wage though, in my opinion, we have to stop feeling responsible for, or pushing social systems to provide for, those who exist below this financial threshold. There will always be some people who choose not to participate in work, or only spottily participate, even in low-paying jobs. I don't believe that any social reform can or will change the fact that some people will still choose not to work hard and/or to live at a low level.

What, you might ask, does this social op-ed have to do with a book on personal finances? Well, as I mentioned in the introduction, I believe that, when we think about personal finances, we cannot assume anything. People and their financial positions do not exist only on one end of the scale of prosperity. There are affluent people in our world *and* poor people, and a whole range in between. For a significant portion of our population, any discussion of personal finances must start with the concept of work, and how it might be understood at the more modest ends of the financial spectrum.

In looking at perceptions and attitudes toward work, we will find people who are unwilling to work or may only work minimally or spottily. I'm not referring to oppressed, downtrodden, or homeless folks. I'm referring to people, like my father, who simply don't care much for work, or whose version of work may result in income so meager that it hardly constitutes an income. And, more critically, the attitude of those people towards work makes all the subsequent discussion in this book about work and income moot.

So, the first rule of successfully managing your personal finances is to work. You, as a person, choose to work. Make this a commitment to yourself and be a person who works. If you're young, start working now. You can get a work permit when you're about sixteen. Do that and get a job. Start the process of understanding what it means to work, what it means to have your own money coming in. Even if your family has enough money, and even if there is no external pressure to do so, learn the lesson of working early. It will improve your self-esteem. It may also inspire you to value or see the benefits of an education, skills development, or training, especially if your early experiences show you the drawbacks of unskilled, minimum-wage work.

If you are reading this book and are not now working, but hoping to find a magic formula to achieve wealth, it starts here. Get a job. Start working. For money. You cannot master the formula of financial success until you have money to master.

You may have seen television shows, or perhaps read books or listened to motivational speakers or celebrities who suggest fabulous wealth can be attained if you abandon or forego the daily-grind type of work and find a dream endeavor. Visualize it and it will happen! I have read some books like that, from *The Secret* twenty years ago to *You Are a Badass* just recently.

While I strongly believe in managing your thoughts, I just don't know what to say to this type of financial manifest destiny. I suppose for a minuscule percentage of the population, visualizing as a tactic for achieving financial success may work. Instead, I'm going to go out on a limb here and say that most successful people achieve their success through simply working hard. For the very largest percentage of the adult population, the achievement of wealth without effort is a pipedream.

About twenty-five years ago, I read in a book that more millionaires had been made in the dry-cleaning business than in any other single business pursuit. I'm sure this statistic is no longer accurate in today's world, but the lesson has stayed with me. The lesson is that more people become financially successful through honest, unglamorous work than from reckless abandon and following their glitzy dreams. I don't want to be known as a dream-killer, but we have too much of this magical thinking. Too many people feel they're selling out or are losers when they succumb to simply working for a living.

Let's consider five archetypes:

- *The Dreamer*
  Big thoughts, big dreams, but it still doesn't pay the rent. I'm not opposed to people, particularly young people, having big dreams and giving them a shot. Acting, music, art, writing, sports. I'm honestly amazed and awed by talented people. Still, it's a sad fact that having a particular talent or a great idea does not always translate into making money with that talent or idea. If you're filled with a passion to strive for a dream, go ahead. Give it a good shot. Obviously, some people do become successful actors, writers, musicians, or the like.

The Dreamer category includes a wide variety of dream pursuits. Consider the currently popular trend to become an entrepreneur. Some people want so badly for their "idea," their food truck, their shop, their invention, or some other self-employment to pay off. I read a story once about the guy who "invented" the seat belt. He spent his life trying to collect wealth from what he felt was *his* idea. Was it unfair that the courts did not agree? Perhaps, but sometimes you have to just move on.

The hard part for some dreamers is that they may have had a success or two. I think of one-hit wonders in the music world, or actors who had one nice role in a television show, or once-outstanding athletes who as dreamers continue to try to recapture or expand upon that modicum of success or long-in-the-past achievement. They might point to or fixate on others who *have* succeeded and so want to believe that it will happen for them too. These dreamers can spend *years* of their life—years they will never get back—justifying the continued pursuit of the dream. All the while *not* financially productive.

I myself patented an invention and thought I

might have found my own personal golden ticket. The Open Airways Acupressure Pillow. Yep. Gonna be big! Twenty-five million people suffer with sinus issues. Gonna be big. But no, it didn't go big. Luckily, I hadn't quit my day job.

It's okay to dream. It's okay to try. But keep an eye on the balance sheet. At some point if *you* have not translated your dream into a real, steady income, you might have to rethink your dream. If you're 35 years old and have never surpassed the annual income poverty marker from your dream endeavor, I regretfully say that maybe it's time to cut the rocker hair, put aside the painting easel, put your head shots away in a drawer, or close up that garage full of your prototype products. Maybe it's time to embrace your dream as a hobby and get a job to pay your rent.

I know it seems like I'm judging these dreamers very harshly, and that I'm the worst kind of dream buzz-kill. And it's okay if you choose to stubbornly pursue your dream despite a lack of financial returns. Maybe your dream will come true someday, or maybe not. Maybe the pursuit of the dream is gratifying enough for you, and you don't mind that you're not financially successful from it. As I stated earlier, some people will choose to live on the edges of financial security, in this case based on pursuing a dream career.

But this book presents another alternative, one that is neither horrible nor soul-killing. To work productively, to become financially secure, and then find ways to embrace your passion and dreams in your spare time. And, by the way, if you become financially successful enough through work, you may just find you have the resources to enjoy your dream activity more fully, because you don't need your dream to pay your bills.

– *The Uninspired*

Ho-hum. Just the opposite of the dreamer, uninspired workers are simply disinterested in career or monetary success. They find any discussion of work strategy tedious. Trying to talk to this type about work may garner a defensive or exasperated response. "Why do you keep rattling on about careers or making more money?" And this type might grouse that they do *have* a job. In some cases, they might have a job or work they have done for extended periods of time. But for the uninspired worker, employment is often on the edges of the employment spectrum, in other words, for low wages, or under-the-table wages, or intermittent wages. Regardless of the nature of their work, this type cares little about "career" and accepts whatever income comes their way.

The main concern with the uninspired is that they rarely have sufficient income to master the other rules of personal finances. You can applaud their willingness to work, however marginally, but such people rarely achieve financial security over the long term.

– The Sponge

Why work? Another percentage of people just really do not mind living off others: off our social systems, off family members, off lovers, or off friends. In America, we once touted the motto that no one is entitled to a free ride, but now we have many who feel they are entitled. I'm *not* referring here to that small population that is legitimately *unable* to work. Nor do I refer to the significant number of people who have worked hard and now can live off a pension, their savings, or legitimately earned social security, nor those lucky enough to have inherited wealth and therefore don't need to work. I refer here to people who could and probably should work, but just don't.

This population often has reasons why they cannot work. I heard one woman say that she would have to pay too much of her paycheck for childcare, so she felt working was not worthwhile. I heard another person assert their "requirement" of a level of income that their skill and qualifications most certainly did not justify. Then came the lament, "See, I can't find a job!" Even when a job is accepted, this type will generally find fault with it, continue to complain, and soon decide to quit or will get fired. Yet, in their mind, the fact that they ever worked, however fleetingly, legitimizes their overwhelmingly more common *un*employment.

These able-bodied people choose to then continue to live off the work of others or off our social systems. And if or when their current host cuts them off, their unemployment runs out, they're denied disability or welfare, or they're kicked to the curb by whatever friend or spouse is supporting them, they cry about how unfair life is. Then they cast about looking for some other institution or person to carry them financially.

– *The Complainant*
Call 1-800 I SUE YOU. This type is looking for a big paycheck for little or no effort. I partially blame unscrupulous lawyers, murky laws, and a dysfunctional court system for encouraging this kind of activity, but almost any minor misfortune can become worthy of litigation. A

slip in a drugstore, stress at work, the fallen branch of a hapless neighbor, a fender-bender. This type will always consider a lawsuit as a possible path to income.

— *The Criminal*
That's illegal? Are you sure? Some people feel that dishonestly collecting money, such as disability or workers' compensation, working "under the table" to avoid paying taxes, cheating on taxes, or manipulating income programs like welfare, is perfectly acceptable. Some go so far as to justify embezzling or fraud. They may even joke about or brag about these financial deceptions. But make no mistake: these activities aren't legal and can have criminal penalties.

Of course, there is also a potential for income from more serious crime, including overt wrongdoing to others through stealing, robbing, dealing, or worse.

Sadly, for school-age kids, crime often pays better than mainstream work, and this is how many young people become ensconced in a life of crime. Yet, over the years few criminals become wealthy. For adults, crime provides a very limited career advancement path. Most criminals, in choosing crime as their employment, still end up living low in the long term. Furthermore, exiting the criminal world is often difficult, and when crime is part of your job history, especially if it has involved jail or prison time, you may be burdened with an enduring career handicap.

Those who do make significant money through crime may exceed the income they might have otherwise achieved through legitimate work, but even this comes at a cost. Most career criminals are socially isolated, living in a world unto itself. In this tangled world of crime, scruples are fluid. Forget honor among thieves or mob codes. In the end, the criminal is always at risk for betrayal and jail or prison time.

Choose to Be a Worker

This brings us back to the start of this section. The first rule of personal finances is to work. You. As a person. Choose to work. If you are young, make this a commitment to yourself. Be a person who works. Start now. Get a job. Be grateful for it. Work hard at whatever job you have and do it well. Understand that working is truly the first rule of successful personal finances. With few exceptions, nothing can improve for you financially until you embrace work.

Once you are solidly working and have income, you can consider improving your work situation, and we will talk about that shortly. But before you can improve your work life, you must first have one. It all comes from the very first rule. You must work.

Before discussing improving income, let's take a quick detour into the dating world.

Dating and Work

Single? Hoping to meet and share your life with someone? Let's talk about this in the context of work.

Scenario One: Just imagine that you are in a bar or at a party, and you have just met someone. You think, "Hmm, very attractive!" After a few minutes of fun and engaging banter, you ask, *"So what do you do…?* And they answer: *"Well I'm between jobs right now. I was laid off last year from…."* Right now, as they continue to tell their sad story, walk away. Say, *"Oh, sorry, I see my friend over there…"* Then just walk away. If they ask, *"Hey, can I get your number?"* say: *"You know, I'm not dating right now."*

Scenario Two: *"So what do you do…?"* Answer: *"Well, I'm just working part time right now…."* Walk away.

Scenario Three: *"So what do you do…?"* Answer: *"I'm talking some time off. I want to go back to school and get a degree in…."* Walk away.

Scenario Four: *"So what do you do…?"* Answer: *"Well, you know, I'm trying to be an actor…."* Walk away.

Scenario Five: *"So what do you do…?"* Answer: *"I'm actually waiting for a big settlement on a court case…."* Walk away.

At this moment, are you in love? Will your heart be torn out and your world crushed from losing this person? No. You just met them. You're not the least invested in this person. But they have told you a very significant fact about themselves. They have told you that employment is potentially an issue with them.

I realize this sounds judgmental. But really, now is the time to decide if you want to be in a relationship with this person. It's hard enough when you meet someone who seems to be solid about working and later find out they're actually deficient in work ethic. At that point, you *are* invested. But here we are talking about someone you just met. You need to learn not to allow an attractive face or body or nice personality cloud your good sense. Don't go into a relationship *knowing* they may not be a worker.

"Oh, Sue, anyone can be going through a bad patch," a friend of mine challenged. True. In the case above, that first person just may find a great new job and be a productive worker starting tomorrow. The person who wants to go back to school could be moving toward a lucrative new career. In the case of that actor, they could strike it big. And the one with the lawsuit might just be in a one-off situation.

But the common thread here is that these are statements from an adult, and adults should be working. With few exceptions, any adult can work. If they aren't working, it's a red flag. You can have a job almost immediately after getting laid off, even if it's an interim job. You can have a second job if one job only offers part-time work. You can have a job *and* go to school. You can have a job *and* still pursue acting (writing, art, music, etc.). You see the point here. These people aren't working. It's a red flag.

And if you proceed to hook up with someone in some version of a not-working situation, you will have only yourself to blame if in a year, or perhaps many years, this person is still not a financially responsible partner. Or, worse, is a financial drain. I'm just suggesting you play the odds and keep looking. It's no hardship to not proceed with a person you don't know.

Here's a real-life case study. Nina quite successfully worked from her home doing accounting. She met Nate online. Nate shared that he was collecting disability due to work-related back issues. Nate admitted he probably could go back to work but felt little pressure to do so, because he had a great doctor who continued to co-sign his need for disability. Instead, Nate was taking time to decide what he wanted to do next as an alternative to his past warehouse-labor career. Sounds okay, right?

After dating for a time, Nate shared that the lease on his apartment had expired and was not being renewed by the landlord. Nate said he was worried about finding another apartment because, as a person on disability, his credit was not great. He also conceded that he needed to return to work to improve his income, and assured Nina that he would be doing so immediately.

The compassionate and somewhat smitten Nina invited Nate to move into her home. It was many years later—I repeat, years later(!)—that this relationship ended finally and badly. Nate never returned to work. He never did contribute financially, and Nina eventually had to legally evict Nate from her home.

Even after sharing that story, my friend told me that I shouldn't judge the romantic choices of others. She chided me saying that it is easy to tell people to use their heads when they meet someone, but many people prefer to follow their hearts or emotions. I maintained that people can and should adhere to some basic criteria for dating, and I stood by the criteria that the prospective party be employed. To which she replied, *"Easy for you to say, Sue. But some people are more romantic about love."*

Here's my response. I've dated many people over the years. Many. I most certainly *have* dated the unemployed. It was not particularly romantic. I've been asked to chip in for dinner or pay for my own movie ticket or provide gas money. Oh, now, don't go getting all judgmental on me. I am no prima donna thinking I need to be wined and dined. I always offer to pay. That's not the point. I just know that, while I may have continued to date that person for a time, financial woes continued to be a central issue, and ultimately those relationships didn't work for me. This comes from my own perspective, that is, the perspective of a working woman. For men, the concern might be about romantic partners who seemed eager to tap their financial resources, who just expected *the men to pay* for everything or to cover all manner of expensive entertainment, food, or gifts.

In my thirties, I embraced a goal of self-betterment——in my finances and career, yes, but also in my relationships. I attended self-help seminars and read many books. Defining what you desire in your life is a basic premise in all areas of self-improvement. It's not unreasonable, nor unromantic, to have some basic standards.

In one seminar, the speaker suggested that the single people write lists of the qualities they want in a life partner. I bet that few people wrote down "unemployed." Now, I suppose some people may want a partner they can take care of, but I suspect most would prefer a mate who is at least somewhat self-sufficient financially. Very few people are looking for a spouse who will mismanage their money or become a financial drain in the relationship. There are many factors that can cause a relationship to fail, but what a blessing if you can minimize or eliminate money management concerns, which are among the most common sources of friction in relationships.

And as a last defense for my recommendation that you not date the unemployed, let me just say that everyone has some criteria for deciding who to date or who not to. *Everyone.* Whatever line you draw in dating, maybe based on age, maybe based on some aspect of appearance, maybe based on current or past marital status, maybe based on religion, you simply cannot say you do not draw a line. Consciously or unconsciously, everyone has boundaries around whom they are willing to date or might choose to walk away from. What I learned after having many disappointing relationships that sometimes dragged on for years is that it is okay, it is even desirable, to adopt healthy dating standards to avoid common relationship issues.

I understand that people are lonely. I get that maybe you don't want to be so practical about relationships, but the risk is significant. You can potentially lose a lot. You might lose your own financial wellness, spend years of your life unhappily, or worse. This is not a high bar to set for yourself, that the people you date must be working. Set this bar as a standard and you may be surprised that you dramatically improve your relationship experiences and possibly have a more secure future. A good work ethic can also be an indicator of other positive qualities in a partner. No guarantees, but this is not bad as a minimum standard.

Improving Your Work Life

I want to make more money.

-Says everyone

Feeling that you need to make more money is not surprising. In doing career coaching, I've heard this expressed more than a few times. I always answer the same way. I always say "*okay*." It's okay to want to make better money than you currently make. Careers are long. The average person will begin working in their teens or early twenties and work until they're in their sixties. That is over forty years. Planning for improvement in income is not a short game but a long one. I always start by encouraging people to keep working and doing well at the job they currently have. Don't quit!

Finding the path to better money is always easier when you're currently making money. Quitting and looking for your next gig makes you a quitter and possibly desperate. It makes you *less likely* to achieve your goal of finding work for better money. However, it's perfectly acceptable to make a responsible career transition.

Responsible Transitions: Quitting or Resigning
What does a responsible transition look like? Well, it never involves a dramatic exit. It's never a burned bridge. It involves no snippy letters or unkind feedback to the boss or the company. Simply give your notice. Thank the current employer for the work they have given you. Leave them wishing you were not leaving. Careers are long. You never know when a former boss or co-worker will come back into play. A burned bridge now can prevent a future opportunity from ever happening.

If you don't have any idea what you might want to do to make more money, I've listed a couple of strategies below that you can try. Keep in mind that careers are long and, if you try something that doesn't work out, you can try something else later.

Another key point is that, with a few exceptions, you can pursue a career doing almost anything, if, of course, you are willing to do the footwork to prepare yourself. Be a doctor; be a lawyer; be an architect; be a scientist. There are steps that can take you to almost any career. It's worth repeating that, if at all possible, you should not abandon your current employment until you have secured your next job. Pursue the development, training, or education you need while you continue to work. And in all cases, make sure you do your current job well.

If you don't enjoy your current employment and have been a lackluster employee up to this point, now is the time to step it up and begin demonstrating your hardest-working self. If your plan includes a hope for advancement or a new role with your current employer, your current manager's good opinion will be critical. You need your manager to support your goal and, if you are hoping to change roles internally, to give you a positive recommendation.

If you plan to leave, even if you're sure you'll be in an unrelated field, you may be surprised to know that your old company's opinion of you can still be a factor in achieving that goal. And, as I said, careers are long; you may at some point need a reference or to take a transitional or interim job to bridge an employment gap. Former employers are good sources of references or as a "back pocket" employment option, but only if the former employer has a good opinion of you. No burning bridges. No abrupt exits. No telling them what you think. Always transition responsibly and professionally.

Getting Fired

Be professional even if they fire you. Always maintain your composure and be gracious at termination. I have been fired. It happens. In one case, though hurt and shocked, and even believing the firing was petty and unfair, I nevertheless managed to maintain my self-control and to be polite during the termination. A few days later I wrote a very carefully worded "thanks for the experience" letter to my ex-boss, with no negativity whatsoever. A year later he called to offer me some consulting work. You never know. Never burn a bridge.

What Do You Want to Do?

When people say they want to make more money, I commonly ask, "*So what is it you want to do?*" The answer, for many, is unclear. Just wanting to make more money is not a career path. Actual career development involves figuring out and making decisions about what you might want to do. Over my career, I have made quite a few transitions. I've also, as part of my role as a training and development professional, helped a number of other people with this process.

Let's start with me. Here's a list of some of the paid jobs I've had:

- Babysitter
- Housecleaner

- Waitress
- Screenplay reader
- Administrative assistant
- Shelf stocker / cashier in retail
- Psychiatric ward tech
- Drug and alcohol abuse counselor
- Teacher (substitute & night school)
- Office furniture salesperson
- Real estate agent
- Corporate real estate owned (REO) sales rep
- Facilities manager
- Corporate training generalist
- Corporate training manager / leader
- Self-employed training consultant
- Writer

You can make up your own list. What have you already done, workwise? Once you have your own list, ask yourself how you felt about each of those jobs. Which jobs or which parts of a job were fulfilling, and which parts were objectionable? When I work on career planning with an individual, in addition to discussing income, we always talk about trying to find a career path that might allow them to do tasks they like doing. A job is always better when you like the work. Still in many cases you will not know with certainty whether you will like a new role or career path. The best you can do is make a plan and see how it goes. In general, however, I remind people that it's surprisingly easy to like a role when you are making excellent money. Right?

In considering how to find work that pays more, let's review a few strategies.

Strategy One: Organic Growth in Role
Start Internally

Always start with looking to your current job situation and asking yourself if there's a role with your current employer for your next move. In your current job, you can leverage relationships with bosses and co-workers who already know you and may help you grow in your career. You can do this even in food service or the humblest of jobs. Ask your boss if there is a career path in your organization where you might do your current work at a higher level? Or is there a management path that involves overseeing your role and others in that role?

Or is there a role within the company but outside your current role that you might want to try? Talk to your boss or other employees to find out what roles exist. But don't expect your boss to have all your development answers. You need to bring ideas and good organizational awareness to the discussion. Look at the titles on phone lists or org charts, if you can get access to them, or review titles and roles on the company's website job postings. Or go on LinkedIn to see what job titles exist in companies like yours. Then talk to your boss or fellow employees about those roles and what people in them do. Your boss or other person you talk with may have suggestions or feedback you should heed.

Many companies, large and small, have assorted departments involving different types of work. Typical departments are shown in Figure 1 below:

Typical Departments in Corporations		
Core Operations / Manufacturing	Sales / Business Development / Account Management	Customer Service / Call Center
Marketing	HR	Accounting/ Finance
Research & Development	Communications	IT
Facilities	Administrative Support	Legal

Fig. 1

To learn more about other departments and roles, you can do some informal internal research when chatting with your boss or co-workers. You can also more formally request a few minutes of your boss's or a co-worker's time to talk about development or a role, department responsibilities, or a job posting. If a role sounds interesting, and the feedback is encouraging, keep that department/role on your target list. If the feedback you receive is cautionary or negative, you don't have to discard the potential role, but stay realistic and take the information you've been given seriously. Perhaps the feedback indicates that you would need significant development, certifications, or education for a role. Remember that careers are long. Consider if you can or want to pursue the required credentials.

Back in the 1990s, when I was doing real estate sales within a company, I saw an internal job posting for a Human Resources (HR) Training Specialist role. I thought I was qualified because I had previously taught school as a part-time gig. I expressed interest and spoke with the hiring manager. That manager gave me a list of development items, including several lengthy ones, such as completing a certification program in organizational development, getting an HR certification, *and getting a master's degree(!)*, among numerous other requirements. At the time I was given the list, I thought, "*Are you kidding me?*" Still, over the years, I completed all of the suggested development items.

The advice the woman had given me was, though daunting, ultimately invaluable. That conversation and my willingness to start checking off those development items led to me eventually being offered the training job long before I had finished most of the suggested development. But it was my willingness to do the work and pursue all those certifications that gave my employer confidence in me. And, importantly, eventually having all those credentials directly qualified me for the *senior* corporate training role I currently occupy and where I am quite well paid.

If you are aspiring to a significantly different role, with potential for a higher income, for example a role that has more potential for advancement, you may first have to consider doing some development activities. Then you might still have to consider a lateral move, or even sometimes a step-down role—essentially, any available role—to enter into the new field. In my example above, when I was finally offered the training role, it actually paid less than my compensation as a salesperson.

Here's another example of someone I knew. After I had been working for numerous years as a training manager, Trish, an HR manager at the company where I then worked, expressed her interest in working in training. What did I say? I gave her the same list of development activities that was given to me. To her credit, Trish too began collecting all the certifications and accepted a role as a training specialist, a step down from her HR manager role. Long term, however, she has had quite a successful career in training.

Don't Be Adversarial

In my career I spent about ten years self-employed as a training and development consultant. I occasionally had assignments to coach employees who filed complaints with a client. If the complaint were a verified legal issue, the action path would be through policy-approved and legally defensible corrections. I tended to be called when the investigation indicated that the complaining employee was just disgruntled, rather than being discriminated against. There was great freedom for me in these coaching scenarios. Because I was a consultant, not a company employee, I could speak frankly to these unhappy employees.

Here I want to take a few paragraphs to share my typical consulting message for employees who use complaints or other coercion tactics to try to win their way with an organization. Strong-arm tactics or complaint-based strategies are more common among the less organizationally savvy employees, so I'm speaking here to those who may not know better.

Fact one: Companies aren't required to offer promotion, advancement, or development to any employee. They don't have to do these things. It's not a legal right you have. You're not entitled to it.

Some people have the misconception that they are entitled to or should be "next in line" for a promotion based on tenure. This is untrue. Promotions, advancement, and development may be offered or not at the company's discretion. This means they can pick and choose to whom they offer these perks. Most often, companies offer development or advancement to employees who—no surprise here—do their job very well. But they are equally entitled to offer a plum role to a favored nephew, or to some less-tenured, less-educated, less-qualified, or less-talented co-worker of yours. This is not illegal. It isn't grounds for a legal complaint. To recap, just because you want advancement or development doesn't mean the company has any obligation to offer these perks *to you*. The management team is legally entitled to offer development or other opportunities to the people they like best. And, to repeat, most often the person they like best is actually one of their best workers. Hence the advice to become one of the best workers.

Fact two: not liking you is not illegal discrimination (unless you can prove that the dislike is verifiably based on some protected status). Nor is it discrimination when your manager or company does things that you do not like (again unless you can prove that those actions are verifiably based on your protected status).

Fact three: If you choose to become adversarial with your boss or your company, you will not be a favorite employee. If you try to pressure your boss, are confrontational, or file a complaint, you are putting a wedge of negativity between you and both your boss and the company. Even the most tolerant of managers or companies will find it hard to like you for it. Using strong-arm tactics within an organization will make management wary of you. If they do try to appease you, and companies sometimes do appease complainers just to avoid legal hassles, this will be done without real enthusiasm for you or your ongoing success. If what I just said about appeasing sounds like a "win" to you. I have no further advice for you. You play by different rules than I do.

Now, if you are truly being discriminated against, provably based on a protected status, such as your race, gender, age, or national origin, and you are truly entitled to some workplace perk you are being denied…. Okay. Go for it. I understand that if no one complains nothing changes, so kudos to any of you who raise your voice regarding real discrimination.

But again, I warn you, a significant percentage of complaints are not about real discrimination but trying to force your boss or company to give you what you want. And trying to get your way by complaining, filing grievances, or threatening a lawsuit is a poor strategy for navigating a career. Some people, as discussed earlier in this section, will choose legal action or threats of legal action over just working and doing their work well.

If you truly do great work, generally the perks will come without coercion being necessary. In the case that you are very talented and doing a great job, and the company does not see your potential, I suggest you take a different tack.

If your current employer is unwilling to meaningfully reward your good work or provide you with a next step or career advancement, plan a transition. Do not try to force them to value you. I have worked for companies that valued my contribution and freely offered me opportunities. I have also worked for companies that accepted my good work but offered me no particular encouragement or development. In the latter case, I stayed a respectable length of time at those jobs, then made a transition. If you are as talented as you think you are, you should have no problem finding a new employer who would absolutely see your value.

Incidentally, if you transition multiple times and continue to feel underappreciated, you might have to do some uncomfortable introspection. When the consistent message you receive from your employers is that your performance does not warrant further opportunities or special rewards, perhaps the problem is not with those doing the rating. You might need to ask yourself whether you are actually bringing stellar performance or have the talent that deserves such consideration. Adjust as needed. I believe that most people have some type of innate talent and can do some sort of work exceptionally. The question is whether the work you are doing taps into *your* innate talent or you are willing to work hard enough to compensate for any gaps and deliver exceptional performance.

Take note if your pattern involves feeling like or presenting yourself as a career victim. Make a commitment to step up and be your bosses' best employee. But if you must transition, remember: never big drama, always a perfectly professional, courteous departure.

Small Companies, Big Opportunities

If you work for a small company, there can be big career opportunities. In most small companies, roles and departments are correspondingly small. In some cases, a single person may perform one or several department roles. As a consequence, on the down side, small companies have infrequent vacancies, and someone might have to retire, or die, for an opening to occur. On the bright side, because each department is small, smaller companies are often open to cross-training and role flexibility. You may not be given the title or the money you desire while learning to perform new tasks or another role, but you can gather skills that may prepare you for that opportunity if and when the company grows or an opening does occur. At worst, you can use the training to prepare for a transition to an improved role in another organization.

Large Companies, Big Opportunities

If you work for a large company, there can also be big opportunities. Roles and departments in large companies may have "entry-level" roles and other programs to facilitate internal moves. Large companies also typically offer internal training and development programs. All the development I mentioned earlier that I completed for my transition into a corporate training role, including a slew of certifications and even my advanced college degree, were all paid for by company development programs. If you find a role that interests you, but that requires some type of certification or degree, ask if the company will sponsor you in that development. Talk to your boss or HR person about development opportunities. Additionally, because large companies usually have a formal application process for internal jobs, feel free to actually apply for positions. Then use the interview as an opportunity to learn what you might have to do to successfully compete for such a role.

Express Interest

Let people in your company know you are interested in taking on new roles. Also stress that you are willing and able to learn. I have spoken to people who felt snubbed when a co-worker was offered an opportunity or advancement. But when I asked if they had applied or expressed interested, what do you think they said?

Say Yes

If you express interest in development or advancement, be ready to say yes to what is offered. I joke with people I do career-coaching with that development opportunities often come to you cleverly disguised as more work. In my own career, when I was still in a sales role, I expressed interest in taking a next step forward in my career. Some months later I was called into my manager's office and "offered" a special project. I was one of about twenty sales reps at the time, and the project was handing sales for a newly compiled portfolio consisting exclusively of the company's troublesome 2-4 unit inventory. I knew it would be grim. What did I say though? I said "sure." My stint doing that project was indeed tough, and I did not feel particularly successful even though I improved sales significantly. The company management, however, respected and rewarded my hard work and willingness to take on the new challenge.

Later, when the sales function was moved out of state, I survived the reorganization and was offered my first corporate HR-training specialist role, the one I had inquired about some time before. I liked the new role right away, and the company helped me continue to pursue the education and many certifications I needed for the Training and Development/HR field. Then, while happily doing this new role, I reiterated my interest in growth and mentioned that I might eventually want to go into management. But, I was happy doing what I was doing. So what happened?

Again, I was called into my manager's office, and again "offered" a new role. This time I was offered a Facilities Manager role, managing a team of five employees. I had no interest at all in facilities. *No interest.* And I liked the training gig. But what did I say? Of course, I said yes. The two years I spent as a facilities manager were extremely educational, though not work I particularly enjoyed. After those two years, based on another corporate reorganization, I finally left that company, but I was able to leverage the manager portion of my title to become a *training* manager. Plus, in later years, I often used stories from that facilities role while training new managers.

Consider another case, Larry who, with only a GED, took an entry-level job within the county park system. Over the years Larry maneuvered up through the ranks in the system and ended up as a senior manager overseeing three large parks and dozens of employees. Promotion came through doing excellent work at each job level, expressing interest in growth, and saying yes to offered opportunities.

When offered an opportunity, say yes. I am not saying that every possible job that comes your way will be a right move. But be very careful about asking for opportunity, then being picky about whether you will take what's offered. Companies like a will-do mindset. You can generally learn from each opportunity and, if need be, make another career transition after a respectable time.

Strategy Two: Target an Industry – New Career Paths
Changing Industries

Maybe you are sure that the industry you're in is not for you, and that there is no role you can apply for or aspire to inside your current company or industry. Okay. Now you must decide what else you can try.

If you have an idea what you would like to do, put together a list of what it takes to do that kind of work. For example, I decided when I was working in an administrative role at a studio in Burbank that being an admin was not enough for me. After applying and being turned down for more elevated roles within "the industry," I decided that I might need to look outside the entertainment field.

I considered what I would like to do. I wanted work that had a potential for high income, based solely on my own efforts and talent, and that did not require a lengthy education commitment. (Ha! Little did I know what would be expected of me later to transition to the HR training role….) I settled on real estate. While still working at the studio, I took a night class. Then I took the real estate exam and passed, all while still working. Before I gave my notice, I secured placement in a real estate office that offered training to new Realtors, *and then* I gave notice at the studio job. All polite. All very professional.

As another example, Sarah, a woman I have now known for many years, shared when we first met that she was not sure if she had graduated from high school. She had been on disciplinary probation at school during her final weeks and boycotted the graduation. When I met Sarah, it was ten years later. She was working for a temp agency and daydreaming about becoming a therapist. The path to that goal started with a call to her high school to find that, yes, she had graduated. Then over the following years, she went to a junior college, and then transferred to a university where she finalized a bachelor's degree. After that, Sarah applied for graduate school and completed a master's degree in a few years. Then she began the arduous process of volunteering during her evenings and weekends as an unpaid group therapist to amass the 2,000 hours of experience she needed to become licensed. She did all these things while continuing to work full time during the day. She was about thirty when we first discussed her question about high school. It then it took her over twelve years to gather all the education, but as of this writing she has been a successful therapist for almost twenty years. She was playing the long game for her career.

Most mainstream career paths are attainable if you just learn what is required and are willing to prepare yourself. Every goal is just a matter of steps. Take a first step. Then take the next step, and so on. Eventually you can end up in the role or career you hope for. You have nothing but time ahead of you. However long the goal will take, just take a first step, and then the next. I simply cannot co-sign the resignation of some who feel that achieving a better financial situation through their own efforts is too hard, beyond them, or impossible.

Turn Left

An old saying is that if you hit a wall, turn left. I have turned left more times than most. At one point in my mid-twenties, I started taking classes toward a master's degree in psychology to become a therapist. At the same time, I took an entry-level job working as a "tech" in a psychiatric hospital and was later promoted to counselor. Thankfully, I realized quite quickly that I was not suited to work in the psychiatric field. I was unable to offer sufficient compassionate support to the clients and was disheartened by their troubles. I was able to make a quick career adjustment without spending too many years on an incompatible career path.

That was when I took the admin job at a studio. My great idea at that time was to navigate toward becoming, I hoped, a successful screenwriter. To my credit, I did have a completed screenplay to show, but the screenwriting did not pan out for me. The reviews of my writing were brutal, and the studio admin job, as I mentioned above, was not my dream work. So, I got a real estate license. Then, after a few years as a realtor in a challenging economic environment, I accepted a job doing real estate sales within a corporation. Later, as already shared, I took steps to work in the corporate Training and Development/HR field.

You are allowed to make changes. Careers are long, and changes are part of the navigation you might have to do to find financial stability and career satisfaction. Just make sure that every job you try teaches you about what you like and don't like, what you can or cannot do, and what you want to do or don't want to do.

And of course, *always* work.

Have a Plan B

This is critical for financial and career plans. You should always have a Plan B. Not every career shift works out. Understand that you very likely will need a Plan B at one or more points in your career.

Having a backup plan for work is common sense, but like other parts of managing finances, many average people don't have a Plan B. Especially when planning a transition ask yourself, *"What will I do if this doesn't work out?"* Look at my wide-ranging job history, and you can see that not every career move is successful. You may start a new job, or start doing a different kind of work, and find that the "fit" isn't good. The manager or the company might not like you; you might hate the work or the company. In fact, changing companies or getting a promotion, are two of the highest-risk events that can cause career "derailment." Always ask yourself, what will you do if things do not turn out as hoped? Don't be a career victim. Instead have a Plan A and a Plan B: if it doesn't work out, I will... what?

By the way, the answer to that question is not to join the ranks of the unemployed. Over my life, my Plan Bs have included interim work as a waitress, stocking shelves at a department store at night, being an on-call temp employee, substitute teaching, and selling office furniture. All of which I did for periods of time when another career option was not working out as planned. *Always* have a Plan B.

Back-Pocket Skills

Keep the skills required by jobs you can do but might not want to do in your back pocket. For example, I worked as a waitress for over twelve years, sometimes as my primary employment and in later years as a night job. Though I have not needed to do so in nearly thirty years, I still maintain that I could always get a waitress job if I needed to. It's one of my back-pocket skills. I could also teach. Strangely, I love training but did not love teaching school. But I've done it and could do it again if needed.

As another example, Jason, a young person I know, started working in a supermarket during high school and continued for many years thereafter. At one point, Jason decided that even as a department manager in a supermarket, he wasn't happy or making enough money. He transitioned into truck driving. He likes it, but when we chatted recently, I pointed out that within the next ten years or so, truck driving as a career may be challenged by self-driving vehicles. We talked about him having the supermarket skills in his back pocket, just in case. He is also putting together another Plan B, because he would really prefer not to go back into supermarket work. That's how you do it. No blinders. No victims. Have a Plan B and keep some options in your back pocket.

Titles and Hierarchy of Roles in Business
While titles may not matter in some businesses, for example in self-employment or small business situations, in larger companies and corporations understanding the hierarchy of titles can be very instructive (see Figure 2). Personally, I had no clue whether a director or VP was higher when I began working in the corporate world, nor did I realize the quite sizeable variation in income potential for the various levels. I knew that people in management most likely made more money than I did, but I really did not know the actual hierarchy, even as I spent years working in corporate roles. So, when planning and navigating your career, understanding the steps of hierarchy is helpful knowledge, especially if you are currently working in or aspire to work in and advance in traditional organizational structures. Note that smaller companies and some industries are liberal in giving elevated titles, but the corresponding money may be lacking.

Level	Description	Examples	Money Prospects (2020 numbers, rounded)
Manual laborer (blue collar)	Roles include factory work, construction or trades labor, grounds keeping, or any other work that involves some level of physicality in tasks and does not require any special formal education. Particular skills or certifications may be required or desired.	Machine workers, pick 'n' pack workers, construction laborers, trade laborers, drivers, mechanics, restaurant workers, agricultural laborers.	From minimum wage to quite respectable wages. Paid hourly. Some roles have unions with defined income levels. Entry level might only provide income in $25,000 range, while experienced workers get closer to $40,000. Generally labor jobs are topped out at the national median income of about $63,000.
Artisans	Roles include all arts and may or may not involve formal education or training.	Artists, musicians, actors, designers, crafters. Often work "pro tem" on gigs or independently.	Income ranges from sub-poverty levels to extremely well paid. Average income for fulltime working artisans = $53,000.
Small business owner	Owners may actually be doing the work for their business or hire others to do the work.	Includes franchises, cafes and food trucks, boutiques, trade or business services.	Average income of established small business owner = $71,000, as drawn from business proceeds.
Administrative	Office administration roles, utilizing clerical and technology skills. Generally, the lowest tier in a corporation. Note that administrative roles in the corporate world are considered "below the line," and "jumping the line" up to professional level roles can sometimes be a difficult jump.	Receptionist, administrative assistant, office coordinator, accounting, payroll or filing administrators or clerks, mail room clerks, building attendants.	From minimum wage to quite respectable wages. Generally paid hourly. Average income = $32,000.

Professional non-managerial	Work based on education or special training.	Specialist, analyst, consultant, or representative titles, process or project management titles (add department to title, for example, HR Specialist, Research Analyst, Sales Consultant, Account Rep etc.) Plus, teachers and other knowledge workers and some independent self-employed or contract professionals.	Typically, professional incomes average at just above the national median at $67,000. Lawyers, doctors, scientists, or other highly educated professions may see double the median or more.
Supervisor / line manager	First level supervisors, often coming from field positions or specialist roles. Typically involves overseeing the work of subordinates.	Foreman, Lead, Supervisor, and sometimes Manager titles. Add department (Construction Lead, Retail Operations Supervisor, Payroll Manager).	Sadly, first-tier manager roles may pay less than professional roles. $50,000 is average, as many first-tier are elevated from manual labor. Professional line managers do better at $74,000 on average.
Senior manager / director	Department or functional managers or directors. May or may not involve having direct reports. May simply reflect level of role contribution.	Manager or Director of … add department or role to title (Training Manager, Director of Customer Service, etc.)	Incomes at this level vary greatly. Mid-level manager average income is $85,000 and average director level is $125,000.
VP	VP is generally considered an executive-level position. Usually involves managing of subordinate-level professionals, but not always.	VP of … add department or role to title, as above. Sometimes elevated to a senior VP, or executive VP, or somewhat diminished as an AVP, an associate or assistant VP.	Incomes again vary widely, but average income for VP level is $160,000, and usually includes bonuses and other compensation perks.
Senior Executive	Top executives in any organization. But meaningfully top tier in traditional corporations.	C-level roles, such as CEO, CFO, CIO, or other "Chief" role, plus President roles. And occasionally an EVP or SVP role that is truly a top executive for a company function (versus just an elevated VP title).	Incomes of top executives vary as well, but at the lowest end are $185,000 and many are compensated at the multi-million-dollar level.

Fig. 2

Be aware that certain industries have their own special hierarchies and pay ranges, for example, medicine, law, education, government, the military, and the sciences. If you are employed in one of these areas or aspire to be, you will have to decipher the hierarchy of roles and titles, and the typical income associated with them, on your own. Why do this? Because you want to have a good vision of your possible career paths and know where a chosen path might take you.

Important career navigation knowledge also involves knowing where you are at relatively in compensation. Seventeen percent of US households make 25K or less, and flirt precariously with the US poverty marker, which is just under 13K for individuals and 21K for a family of three. Another twenty percent of households earn under 50K. Under 50K is a very modest income in today's world. Almost *twenty-nine percent* of US households earn over 50K and under 100K. This is a reasonable income goal for any US worker. Another fifteen percent earn between 100K and 150K which is also not an extravagant income goal. The remaining eighteen percent earn over 150K annually.

Understand Compensation for Work
Why bother explaining workplace compensation? Because knowing what might be offered, or knowing what might be requested or negotiated, in your work compensation is part of financially educating yourself for career success. In my early work years, I did not assess my compensation; I was just happy to be employed. I knew

nothing about salaries or income levels, and certainly nothing about other, more sophisticated varieties of compensation such as bonuses or benefits . I evaluated jobs solely on the hourly wage or salary and took what was offered.

However, depending on the type of work you do, compensation actually varies considerably. And again I admit that until I was in actual roles that changed my compensation I had no idea that there was such variation in pay.

So, let's review the most commonplace compensation schemes and then a few compensation considerations that are less typical.

- *Hourly Pay*
  Many, if not most, people spend some portion of their careers doing work where they will be paid an hourly wage. In the US, the Department of Labor puts the percentage of American workers who are paid hourly at 59%. In legal HR terms, this is usually referred to as "non-exempt" work because the pay is *not* exempted from overtime eligibility. If an hourly paid worker works more than forty hours in any given workweek, they *will be* eligible for overtime. Note that some states specify other parameters for allocation of overtime. For example, in California overtime kicks in if the person works more than eight hours in a given day. Federally, however, the mandate for overtime pay is after 40 hours in a workweek. US laws provide for all workers to receive overtime compensation unless they are exempt. We

will discuss exempt pay in a moment. Hourly pay can range from minimum wage, currently about $7.25 federally (2021), to quite respectable dollar amounts per hour. There are some limited cases where a role might pay less than minimum wage. For example, in some restaurants, servers are paid less than minimum wage due to the assumption that they will receive tips in amounts that will make their total compensation over the minimum. On the other end of the spectrum, some skilled hourly paid laborers may command $40, $60, $80 per hour or more. If the job commonly involves overtime, which is paid at 1.5 times the base hourly rate, the income can be quite good overall. Lawyers and other professional consultants, such as therapists, often charge by the hour and might bill clients at hundreds of dollars per hour.

— *Salary*
Being paid a salary versus being paid hourly is also quite common. Salaries are typically presented in annual numbers. The employee is paid weekly or biweekly, but the compensation is simply the annual amount equally divided by the number of pay periods. With very few exceptions, if your role is salaried, you will be "exempt" from overtime, that is, *not* be eligible for overtime pay. The law, however, specifies that the nature of your work must qualify for an "exemption" in order to be exempt. Common exemption categories include professional work that

requires independent judgment, higher education or that is knowledge-based, or work that is managerial. The exemptions are quite specific, and laws also mandate a minimum compensation level. So, your job *cannot* be classified as exempt, thus preventing you from collecting any overtime pay, and be low-paying to boot.

In corporate roles, there can be snobbery regarding those who are paid hourly versus salaried. Hourly work requires tracking, and therefore timekeeping, signing in and out of work, and more attentiveness to arrival, departure, and break times. Salaried or exempt employees do not need to track their time, because they will be paid the same amount no matter how many or few hours they work.

On the flip side, when a salaried employee puts in long hours, as they might often have to, there is no fat paycheck coming to them as compensation for the extra hours. Still, salaried workers tend to feel that being salaried is an elevated status. This snobbery persists even at the lower end of the salary spectrum, despite the fact that a non-exempt worker might actually make as much or more money, considering hours worked with overtime pay.

If you are being offered a salary versus hourly wage employment, there may be room for negotiation. Many companies build in a small variance or allowance for possible negotiation after an initial salary offer is made. I understand that many workers don't feel confident enough to negotiate wages or salaries. I've coached numerous people during career transitions and had more than one later admit they felt too uncomfortable to counter an initial offer from a new employer.

But here is the thing about doing so. In most companies you might hope to get a 3% raise annually, more or less. Asking for a modest improvement to any initial offer for employment, which *is* a generally accepted process, can secure for you one, two or more years' worth of raises. The worst that will happen will be a declined request or a lesser counteroffer. Since most workers will transition at least a few times, and some will transition a dozen or more times, developing the confidence to make a reasonable request in response to an employment offer can translate into thousands of dollars of better compensation over your lifetime. The key, of course, is to ask respectfully and reasonably. For a $50,000 annual salary, a counteroffer of $55,000 translates into a 10% difference in salary, which would take you *years* to achieve via a 3% annual increase. Even if they counteroffer at $53,000, you would be collecting a two-year raise in advance.

- *Bonuses*

  I honestly did not know anything about bonuses until I was transferred into my first job as a manager, and the offer letter indicated I would be eligible for a 10% annual bonus. Cool, I thought. I was unaware that managers in most traditional companies receive bonuses. I had worked in the studios in my twenties, and I am sure bonuses were commonplace there, but my roles were always paid hourly. So, who knew?

  Bonus percentages range from 10% for lower levels of management (or even some high-level individual professionals) to well over 100% for executive levels. Sometimes the bonus is tied to a specific performance metric, such as business or individual performance. Most bonuses are awarded annually, but bonus structures do vary. If you are considering or aspiring to a management path, you'll want to investigate how your target company or industry handles bonuses. Bonuses are one of the very nice perks of advancing into management or higher-level titles in a traditional organization.

- *Commission*

  Commission pay is generally associated with sales roles. Many types of sales involve "straight commission." This means there is no other pay, just commission. Commission amounts are based on either a percentage of the sale amount or some other defined dollars-for-sales computation. When companies pay only straight commission, the hope is that the salespeople will be highly motivated to deliver, since they only receive compensation if they complete sales. Sales roles can be very lucrative, but not every person can handle the pressure and responsibility of managing their work activities to hustle leads and close deals. I sold real estate in the traditional sense for a few years, and it was tough. I also sold office furniture part time, when I was getting started in real estate. Both were 100% commission-based. Frankly I found the office furniture sales, with its on-going business relationships, a bit easier, though ultimately not as lucrative.

Later I worked in REO (real estate owned) sales in a corporate setting. In that environment, I received a base salary plus commission for my sales. In some commission-compensation structures the salary portion of the income, though usually low, can be ongoing, as it was in my role. But in others, the base or salary pay is considered a "draw," that is, an advance against future sales. Working in real estate, as I did for many years, in resale, REO, and later in new home sales, I have seen countless salespeople wash out because they had no idea how accountable they would be for generating sufficient sales to earn adequate commissions. Though sales can be and often is high-paying, you must determine if you are suited to the concept of no set or guaranteed income.

If you are considering commission work, be sure to ask about and understand the pay structure and expectations.

— *Benefits Package*
When considering a job or career path, you might also want to carefully assess the value of the likely benefits that are being offered. A benefits package that includes free or deeply discounted health insurance, life insurance, short-term and long-term disability insurance, paid holidays and vacations, or other wellness benefits has real value. While you might not miss having some of these benefits if you choose self-employment or decide to work for a small private company without benefits, don't deny their value. With many companies, a cushy benefits package represents thousands of dollars in real value being given to you annually as part of your compensation. While going without these benefits can sometimes be of no consequence, *most of us* know of someone who, for example, has experienced some type of injury or illness that dramatically altered their job situation, or have friends that lament that they cannot afford to take time off because their income stops when they do not work. When hearing these friends or family talk you might realize that having paid vacation, good health insurance or disability insurance is a truly valuable benefit.

— *Pension Plans*

Once upon a time, most large and many smaller companies offered their employees pensions if they worked for the company for a minimum number of years. A pension is a lifetime monthly income once you retire. The monthly amount paid out would be based on a percentage of your annual income while working for the company, and that percentage would increase based on your years of service. Voluntary retirement savings, that is, 401(k)s, discussed below, have largely replaced pensions in traditional businesses, shifting the burden of preparation for retirement squarely onto the employee's shoulders.

In defense of the companies that have moved to discontinue pensions, funding and management of such a benefit has in the past twenty or thirty years become unsustainable. People live longer and stay with companies for shorter stints, and administration of a pension fund is quite burdensome. Furthermore, employees have been generally unwilling to help offset the rising costs of pension programs with personal withholdings from their compensation.

This is not to say that pensions are not available in any career. Today the typical career paths that offer pensions are governmental. This group is much broader than you might imagine: from local, state, or national park workers, to public school teachers and staff, to career military personnel, to law enforcement, to community services such as fire departments and all assorted city, state or national government administrative or social -service employees. One drawback of government pensions is that since you are accruing a government pension, which is technically government money that is paid to you in retirement, a portion of the social security benefits you might normally be eligible for will be excluded. This is not as unfair as it might seem, as while you are working in a government job most often you do not contribute to social security.

Pension Buyouts

A common practice with corporate pension programs is to offer a cash buyout of the vested benefit. Employees are offered a lump sum, sometimes a handsome amount, to forfeit the monthly payments they would otherwise receive in retirement. The unsuspecting employees are coached that if they invest the lump sum, they would likely reap more dollars overall than the possible monthly benefit would provide over a typical retirement. Companies offer this alternative because pensions are, as already mentioned, so difficult to administer and so costly.

There are, however, problems with buyouts. Too few employees are disciplined enough to put the buyout dollars in an appropriate retirement fund and leave it there. Any portion of the funds not so placed will become immediately taxable, so there goes a large chunk of your proceeds. Plus, future earnings are lost, of course, and at that point you have no retirement benefit from the pension. Zilch.

I was offered such a payout by one company I worked for early in my career. My "pension" was only estimated at $275 to $450 per month, depending on my age when I applied to begin receiving benefits, not a very substantial income. Still, I declined the buyout. Instead, I did a few calculations and decided to start collecting the benefit at the earliest eligible age. I now direct-deposit the pension dollars into an online savings account that offers decent interest, and every time the account reaches $5,000, I open a CD for that amount. If I do not touch the deposits, and I have not yet, I estimate I will have accrued about $30,000 in after-tax dollars by the time I plan to retire. $30,000 is more than the buyout amount I was offered. And I can spend those dollars without owing taxes, while still having that small pension income for the rest of my life.

Buyouts make great sense for companies. Most often the buyout does not make the same good sense for the employee. The buyout pitch, however, may be quite hard sell. You may have to stand firm to decline. Regulations do require, in most cases, the alternative of preserving the pension, though the pension may be transferred and administered by a third party, particularly if the company's pension fund is being disbanded.

— *401(k) Retirement Accounts*
Virtually all large companies and many smaller ones offer their employees a voluntary retirement saving option, typically a 401(k). While just offering employees a place to put away some pre-tax dollars for retirement is a good and valuable benefit all on its own, many companies go much farther with retirement savings accounts. Often the company *will match* a portion of the funds you put into the offered 401(k) retirement account, typically 3 to 6 percent. Matched dollars are a cash benefit that should never be forfeited. Always sign up for at least the offered matched percentage wherever you work. 401(k)s are discussed in more detail in section four.

Matching funds is actual compensation to the tune of 3% to 6% in whole dollars, that is, in dollars given to you without taxes being taken out. And, like the dollars you put in, you will receive returns or gains on those whole dollars while they are in the retirement account. Just a note that generally you will not "vest" or own the dollars from the company's match until you have stayed with the company for a few years. This may be a good reason, whenever possible, to give any company a few years of your career time, even if you decide that the company or career path is not for you. When you leave before vesting you may, potentially, be walking away from thousands of dollars. Remember, careers are long; you don't need to be in a hurry to make a transition. Plan your next move, and time the transition to make the best financial sense for you.

Another important feature of a 401(k) is that your funds, and even the matching funds that your employer contributes, are protected. These protections were put in place to keep employees' retirement funds safe, as pensions have become less and less common. Of course, 401(k)s are investment programs, so they do have investment risk as we will discuss in the investment section, but the dollars in these accounts cannot be tapped by creditors if your organization fails, and all the funds, including any vested matching funds are safely yours if you leave your company. Because of these protections and stipulations, 401(k)s also have contribution limits. As of this writing in 2021, the limits are about $19,500 annually, plus another $6,500 if you are over fifty, as catch-up contributions. You can usually add additional dollars to your 401(k), but once you meet the pre-tax limits your contributions will be from after-tax dollars. An employee with a salary of $150,000 can max out their 401(k) with a 12-16% pretax contribution, depending on whether catchup contributions are being set aside.

— *Expense and Allowances Compensation*
Depending on your role, the company, or the industry, you may be eligible for other nice little compensation perks. Among the most common are:

- *Cars or car allowances.* Roles that require the use of a vehicle can and do usually provide either the vehicle or an allowance for the wear and tear on your own vehicle. This may be handled on a flat allowance basis or be based on logged mileage.

- *Parking allowance or free parking.* Don't laugh. Not every company offers employees a free place to park. And in some locations, parking can be very costly.

- *Public transportation assistance.* Relating to the challenge of parking or due to a commitment to environmental responsibility, some employers offer a stipend or reimbursement for the use of public transportation.

- *Mobile phones.* When needed for work, a mobile phone may be provided by your employer, usually allowing you to use that phone for your personal needs, and thereby saving you the cost of a mobile phone. As an alternative, more and more these days, companies provide an allowance for your own personal device when it will be used for some work needs under a BYOD (bring your own device) program.

- *Travel expenses.* Whenever you must travel for work, companies generally provide reimbursement for all reasonable travel expenses. This includes airfare, hotels, rental cars and gas, and your food expenses while traveling. My training career sometimes requires extensive travel, and while I am on the road, all my meals are billed to my employer, despite the fact that they do not pay for any of my meals when I work from the office. This is typical in business travel, though some companies have a daily dollar limit called a "per diem." Still, I consider my travel expense reimbursement a perk. During the time I'm on the road, I'm not paying for food or gasoline, so that is a savings to my budget.

- *Tuition reimbursement.* Many companies, particularly larger corporations, offer tuition reimbursement for college or other educational programs. In some cases, you are required to have been employed for a designated time, such as one or two years, before you are eligible. Additionally, some employers require that the educational pursuit be aligned with your job role at the company or approved as part of a developmental plan. But, in many organizations, there are few restrictions. If pursuing a college degree or other certification is part of your career plan, this perk can be extremely valuable. If tuition assistance is offered by your organization, I suggest you think hard about utilizing it, even if you are not being pushed or encouraged to pursue career development. Do it because, one, they are giving you the perk of free or nominally priced education, and two, having additional education or certifications can translate into higher wages for you for the rest of your career.

- *Relocation assistance.* If you are looking at a job in another city or state, even if it's with the same company where you already work, a relocation package may be offered. Packages usually provide for a defined number of trips back and forth, temporary housing cost while in the new city, rental car cost until settled in the new location, moving company fees, including the fee(s) to transport your car(s), travel for family, and sometimes assistance with the selling of your old house or purchasing a new one. Note that most relocation packages will stipulate that the money is given, but your employment must successfully continue for a designated period of time after the move, often one or two years. Otherwise, you may need to reimburse your employer some of that relocation money. If the employer dismisses you, however, they usually waive any required reimbursement.

- *Employee discounts on products or services.* If you work for a company that manufactures a product, you may be offered deep discounts on that product or products used in the purchasing pipeline. Your ability to utilize the products or discounts may be somewhat serendipitous, but worth exploring. In some cases, substantial dollars may be available if your ability to utilize them is aligned.

- *Onsite gym or gym membership.* Having the ease of visiting a gym right at your workplace, especially if free, is a great perk, and not just a financial one. A gym membership can be helpful too, particularly if you already regularly visit a gym.

- *Onsite childcare.* Pretty rare, but very valuable for employees with small children.

— *Hiring Bonuses*

Once common, in more recent years, post-Great Recession, hiring bonuses are less so. Still, for prized talent or in highly competitive roles, or to lure talent away from a current employment situation, a hiring bonus may be offered. Dollar amounts vary widely from a few thousand dollars to many tens of thousands. Most commonly, the hiring bonus will be based on some known factor, for example, the dollar amount of a candidate's upcoming but forfeited bonus amount at their former company.

— *Stock Options*

I learned about stock options long before I was ever in management. because I worked for a company that offered stock options to all employees. More commonly, stock options are offered by companies to managers and above, or in some cases only to executives. Here's how it works. You are awarded a number of stock share options, which must then mature, meaning you can't cash them out until "x" date. Usually, options mature in a year or more. Assuming the stock price rises, and the hold period has passed, you can then use your option to either purchase the shares at the earlier, lower price or cash them out.

Of course, the hope is that the company will perform well, and the stock price will rise. This is the value, in fact the only value, of the options. So, stock options only have value if the company's stock goes up. Many executives in the country have vast quantities of worthless stock options awarded when the company stock was riding high, but which would result in a loss if redeemed when the stock is trading much lower. You may have heard of scandals in some businesses over stock options. Some high-profile businesses have been caught "post-dating" stock options for their executives to create scenarios where the exercising of the options will translate into lucrative profits. This is illegal, of course. The option is offered based on a stock price at a given time, and only to be exercised per the maturity stipulations in the offer.

— *Long-Term Incentive Compensation*
Long term incentives (LTIs), also sometimes referred to as retention bonuses, may also be offered as part of a compensation package for an executive or senior manager. These are bonuses that are not payable unless the executive is still employed by the company when it "matures," usually some years down the line, with three or five years being common. The nice part of LTIs is that the money is not usually contingent on any criteria other than still being employed at the future date. The company's or individual's performance is not generally a factor.

— *Deferred Comp*
Deferred comp (aka deferred *compensation*) simply refers to money taken from your gross income *before* taxes and placed into a savings/investment account. With deferred comp, as with a 401(k), you can reduce your annual income tax bill by lowering your reported income. Deferred comp is not reported as income, at least not until the dollars are withdrawn. While this is the same benefit as received from a 401(k), there are some significant differences between a 401(k) and a deferred comp plan.

A deferred comp plan, like a 401(k) is offered as a way to save and also a way to shield a portion of your current income from taxes. Because of the contribution limits put onto 401(k)s, an employee with a salary of $150,000, as already mentioned, can max out their 401(k) with a 12-16% pretax contribution, depending on whether catchup contributions are involved.

Highly compensated employees, then, can often max out the possible 401(k) contribution and still have spare funds available and a desire to save (and to lower their annual tax bill). A non-qualified tax-deferred compensation plan, commonly referred to as "deferred comp" (typically a 409A plan) now enters the picture. A non-qualified plan allows an employee to contribute *up to 100%* of their annual income, but most programs specify a somewhat lower cap. Because it is a non-qualified plan, versus a 401(k) plan which is a qualified, highly regulated retirement plan, deferred comp plans have fewer protective provisions, and might, for example, require automatic cash-out upon termination with the associated potential tax consequences. Furthermore, the funds in a deferred income account remain at risk, and could be seized, should the organization fail. If a company transition is likely for you within a few years, or if the organization is under duress, you might think twice about participating in this "perk."

— *Severance Packages*

When companies "let you go," particularly if the dismissal is "no fault," that is, not for any particular cause, or related to a reduction in force (RIF), impacted employees are often offered a severance package. In fact, substantial packages are typical for executives or higher-level managers who are asked to amicably depart, even if this is based on perceived underperformance. At the highest levels, the severance package is sometimes referred to as a "golden parachute."

For average employees, a severance package commonly includes a flat dollar amount which may be based on years of prior service, and a period of bridging of health benefits coverage. In exchange for the package, the employee usually agrees to sign an agreement with a "hold harmless" clause, in effect saying that the company is not doing anything wrong, and the employee agrees not to pursue legal action based on the dismissal. In some cases, the package is standardized and unalterable, but in others you might be able to request a somewhat improved package, particularly, for example, if you are just shy of getting a substantial bonus or LTI. At high levels, the severance dollars are substantial, and negotiation can result in significant adjustments to the initial offer. Companies usually really want that signed waiver, and, though you want to conduct the negotiation respectfully, they are in fact dismissing you, so it is okay to be a little less cordial in your negotiation strategy.

Interviewing, Negotiation, and Organizational Savvy

It is wise to learn about and fair to ask about all the possible compensation offered in any job you are considering. When transitioning, it is also fair to do some negotiation on compensation, as already mentioned. But before you start negotiating or asking for any compensation adjustments, you should first understand what's typical and what's possible. Asking for a level or type of compensation that isn't possible or reasonable demonstrates a lack of organizational savvy. The result may be no offer of employment or an offer being rescinded.

As important as what you ask is who you ask and when. It's generally *not* advisable to attempt to probe compensation details with the hiring manager in your job interview. Really. Don't do it. While the manager may know the compensation possibilities, they are interviewing you to determine if you are a good candidate to do the job. Raising the issue of compensation in an interview, other than in very general terms, raises a red flag for the hiring manager. Instead of assessing your value, the hiring manager may be led to ponder if you will be continually confrontational about your compensation. Treat the interview as a stand-alone event, solely to demonstrate your ability to do the job. Really. No compensation challenges.

On the other hand, if you have the opportunity to speak with a recruiter or an HR rep that works with the company or in the industry you are exploring, they are often very knowledgeable about what's possible and what's not on the table. They *are* the right people to ask. Most often the compensation range for a job is presented in the initial contact, in what is called a "screening call." This is an acceptable time to ask a few questions, but not a time to attempt to negotiate. The time to negotiate is once they like you and want to hire you. On the screening call you can respond honestly to the salary or pay range they provide. If the pay is not acceptable, do not waste their time or yours thinking you will be able to negotiate the compensation up to a workable level. I have had calls from lots of recruiters over the years, and most often the call ends based on the clearly too low salary for the role. The trick with salary/pay negotiation is to be in the right ballpark from the start. Then, after you have been interviewed and they really want to hire you, you can ask to be on the higher end of their range.

In my own career, I have sometimes just accepted job offers, as I mentioned at the start of this section. But as I became more savvy about compensation, I secured, in various jobs I accepted: a hiring bonus, immediate eligibility for tuition reimbursement for the last leg of a master's degree, a monthly car allowance, indoor parking structure parking (in Denver—no scraping off snow, thank you), enhancements to a relocation package, and of course the occasional small bump in salary. With compensation, first learn what might be on the table, again particularly when you speak with recruiters or HR representatives, then ask for reasonable improvements. And, importantly, consider non-salary possibilities in your calculations. By the way, sometimes you can just ask if there is anything else the employer might be able to offer to sweeten the compensation package. In my case, this strategy led to an unexpected monthly car allowance in one transition to the tune of about $5,000 annually.

Strategy Three: Going It Alone
Self-Employment

I cannot deny that there are many career paths outside traditional employment with a company. Small business ownership, self-employment, partnerships, gig or contract work can be lucrative or not. You have to ask yourself if you are suited to this type of work and recognize that there can be significant drawbacks in terms of personal finances. I worked for several years as a real estate agent, which means I was essentially self-employed. Later I worked for ten years as a consultant, so again, self-employed.

Figure 3 outlines some of the pros and cons of non-traditional careers:

Self-Employment	
Pros	**Cons**
• Potential for high earnings	• Takes high level of discipline
• Flexibility – you do work you want when you want	• You have to do everything, roles typically taken care of by others, accounting, tax-paying, marketing, etc. are all your responsibility
• Independence – no boss	• Income can be up and down, or spotty
• Personality – not suited to work in traditional role	• No built-in retirement savings plan
	• No company-sponsored benefits, like paid vacation, overtime pay, or health benefits

Fig 3

If independence and flexibility are your goals, then maybe a non-traditional job might be good for you, and the potential for high earnings is there as well. But be realistic. 50% of small businesses fail within 5 years. Among the small businesses that do survive, the average income for owners is only about $70K. Those that gravitate toward non-traditional jobs typically grossly overestimate how much money they will make and underestimate the effort it will take to drum up business. They rarely realize that they must either develop skills in marketing or pay someone to do it for them.

Furthermore, the self-employed and small business owners often face challenges during economic downturns, when regardless of your talent or marketing efforts your business volume may significantly dip. After ten years of self-employment, I chose to take a corporate job. Though I liked the flexibility of being self-employed, I was tired of the ups and downs in income. Additionally, I hated having to sell myself to get new clients. It was like having to go through employment interviews several times a year. Ugh! And though I made decent money, six figures most years, it was still a pay cut from my corporate roles, and did not offer paid benefits, vacations, a retirement account, or any of the other niceties of a regular job. Lastly, I missed the perks I was eligible for as a senior-level manager in a corporate role: sizable annual bonuses, stock options, and long-term incentives.

I have numerous friends and family members that are self-employed. In fact, both of my brothers are self-employed small business owners. Neither of them was suited, personality-wise, for traditional employment, and happily, both found lucrative self-employment alternatives to working for others. Non-traditional can be fine, but again, as mentioned above, it takes discipline. You can make good money. But even if you're good about managing your money, which is the topic of the next rule, it takes real discipline to save and prepare yourself for retirement when you are structuring your own business and/or doing non-traditional work.

It's worth saying here that self-employment can tempt you toward the dark side of keeping income under the table or cutting legal corners. I have had friends who found themselves in financial conundrums by playing free and easy with the legal side of their business or income. Penalties for discovered breaches can be heavy financially. One small business owner friend was audited by the IRS and fined over

80K for improper tax withholding. Another friend was approaching retirement and wanted to sell his business but was hobbled by the fact that a good number of his accounts and employees were "under the table."

Being a Boss

Aspiring to expand a self-employment situation to include hired employees, that is, to become a boss, is another possible career path. You might achieve this through building a small, individual endeavor or through a franchise purchase with a business model that requires employees right from the start. Being a boss is somewhat different than being a manager within a company. On your own, you have to assume all responsibility for the quality of your employee choices. The *Rich Dad/Poor Dad* book series by Robert T. Kiyosaki and Sharon Lechter has some good insight into the challenges of being "the boss" in a cash business. Still, many people find the concept of building a business and having employees deeply appealing. Just know that payroll, accounting, and human resource challenges can be significant. Failure rates for small businesses, as already mentioned, are quite high; 30% fail within two years and 50% within five years.

Passive Income

I was first alerted to the concept of passive income when I worked during my twenties in the entertainment industry. I did an internship in the 1980s where part of my job was tabulating overseas weekend box-office ticket sales for movies. The company was required to track exactly how many tickets were sold and royalties were paid based on those numbers. I was a bit surprised to learn that every time a show or movie aired, whether broadcast or in a theater, a royalty – or residual – payment was due to a wide range of the talent involved in the show. I thought that was a great deal for the talent.

Obviously, being in the talent side of the entertainment industry is one avenue to passive income. I have a neighbor who is not a big star but has worked consistently as an actor in recurring or guest roles on many popular television shows, while doing commercial or stage work in between. He has made good, steady money, raised a nice family and has had a fine, comfortable life. But his income from current gigs is always supplemented to some extent by passive income from residuals. His wife jokes that she has seen residual checks as low as under $1, but especially as one looks to retirement, having any passive income from work that was done in past years, well, that's just a good deal.

The entertainment industry, including music of course, is probably the most obvious career choice that has potential for this type of passive income. Note that only the "talent" or higher level creative roles are eligible for residuals in the entertainment field, not all the many supporting employment roles in those industries.

But entertainment it is not the only avenue to passive income. You can invent a product, have it manufactured, and sell the product. Or you can sell the rights to your product and receive royalties. The royalty is a very small fraction of a percentage that you receive as payment on each and every sale of the product. Similar income potential could come from an app or software program. Sweet. Celebrities or athletes sometimes license their images and receive royalties for toys or other products that use their names or images.

You can also make passive income from writing a book or other creative activity, such as painting or sculpture. While artists can only sell an original work of art once, they can sell reprints or reproductions of their art or license their pieces. They can also put their art on coffee mugs, tee shirts, or other products, reaping repeated rewards from a single creative effort. I've designed training materials that I was able to license and sell to companies for their use. I also developed a deck of "competency cards" to be used in corporate training and HR applications, which I still sell on Amazon.

Sometimes, something you do for enjoyment can have passive income potential. Annie, a friend of mine, had a blog about her two dogs with quite a following. The blog led for a time to many "sponsorships" and some advertising income. All Annie had to do was allow the sponsors or advertisers to post on the sidebar of her blog—and voilà!—passive income from an activity she was doing for fun anyway. Other people create a YouTube channel for their fun videos or "how-to" clips, and similarly sell advertising slots.

I will caution you that not every idea or creative pursuit will pan out and generate enough passive income to become your career. I was not able to grow the sales of my licensed training materials into enough income to live on. As mentioned earlier, a product that I patented and brought to market—the Open Airways Acupressure Pillow—was pretty much a dud. Sometimes you get lucky and have sustained passive income, but most often, passive income is insufficient to replace day-to-day work.

When we get to the sections on saving and investing, we will discuss other types of so-called passive income. Interest, appreciation, and rental income are all often associated with the term "passive income," and certainly they each have a place in understanding personal finances. There are people who might see activities related to the collection of that type of income as their actual job. If they can manage to have an income that covers all their financial needs, good for them. My suggestion in most cases is not to bank entirely on passive income streams, or at least to have a solid Plan B in place if the income stream dries up or takes a wrong turn.

Embracing Ownership of Your Career

In the end, your career is yours to manage. Life will undoubtedly place options before you, and you will have to make choices. Some choices may be easy and turn out well, but others may be difficult or lead to disappointment. Such is the nature of a career. While some find a satisfying career early on and stay at it for most of their lives, I believe most people have to do some trial-and-error career-wise to find work that is both personally and financially rewarding.

You do not need to make big bucks to be financially secure, either. In the final chapter of this book, we review some case studies of people I have known and explore how well their work strategies have done for them. As I mentioned in the introduction to this book, I do not come from wealth. Most of the people I know are average folks. But even average folks can be financially secure, and, as you will see, there are financial successes among these average-income workers. But make no mistake, financial success generally starts with a willingness to work. Embrace the work concept and you will be positioned to succeed with the later rules.

As a final message about work, I want to say that career-wise you almost always have options. Alma, an acquaintance of mine, recently turned forty and is at a career impasse. Some years ago, she quit a job after many years in one field because she found it unfulfilling. Then she briefly tried doing office work. Next Alma tried working independently doing direct sales, and most recently has been subcontracting for an hourly wage from another direct selling vendor, but that work is spotty.

When I suggested that Alma might want to consider exploring a new career path, she implied she was too old to pursue any significant career goal. But here's the deal. Even if Alma decides to go through a training or educational program, and even if it takes five years to complete, she could still have a twenty-year career in a new field. Twenty years! And what's her alternative? Alma makes ends meet, yes, largely due to her husband's steady employment, but together they are making little progress toward a retirement plan. My advice would be the same if she were fifty. I know of a policeman who retired with a full pension after thirty years on the force, *then* went to school to become a registered nurse. He has had almost fifteen years as a practicing ER nurse as of the time of this writing.

The beauty of work is that you can decide what you want to do. You can make a plan to pursue new, improved, or just different work situations. If one decision fails, you can make another one. Often our hesitation comes from internal scripts: I'm not good at school; I'm not creative; I'm too old; no one will hire me. But the truth is you can let go of old scripts and write a new story for yourself career-wise. You really can.

No career victims. Make a plan. Turn left, if needed. Have a Plan B. And always work.

Rule Two: Manage

Know *Your* Money

Later, we will discuss more advanced financial knowledge, but here we start again with the basics. You need to know and understand *your* money. If you have embraced the first rule and are working, you have a known income. Now you have to define your budget and become mindful about your money situation. I get a little horrified when I hear someone say that they don't balance their checkbook or know what the balances are in their accounts. Ignorance is rarely a great strategy for managing finances or building wealth.

Choose knowledge and understanding instead. Make a firm commitment to yourself to always know where you stand financially and live within your income. The starting place for knowing your financial situation is through basic balance-sheet accounting. You don't need fancy tools to have a basic balance sheet. A piece of paper with a line drawn down the middle will do. On one side, you'll indicate income; on the other side, you'll indicate expenses.

On the income side, write the "take-home" dollar amount from your paycheck. If you are paid twice a month, write it twice. If you are paid bi-weekly, still write it twice. If you are married, add your spouse's income as well. Also indicate if you have other regular income, such as child support or alimony. Now add up your income.

Next, on the expenses side, start with an amount for your housing cost, rent, or mortgage. Next add an amount for your car payment(s), if any, car insurance, cell phone, and average utility bills (gas, electric, cable, wifi). Add any student loan debt you must pay. If you have a child support obligation, add that as well. These are called fixed costs because you must pay a fixed amount every month.

Next, consider food and essential supplies. What does your usual trip to the supermarket cost? Now multiply that number by how often you typically go to the market each month and add that number to your expense column. Next, think about how often you go out to eat, whether it is for coffee, breakfast, lunch, or dinner. What does a typical coffee, breakfast, lunch, or dinner cost you? Then multiply the various numbers by how often you purchase those meals and put that tallied number into your expense column. Finally, consider what you commonly pay for gasoline or other transportation. Multiply the typical cost of a tank of gas, times the usual number of fill-ups per month. Or if you use other transportation, estimate those costs and add them to your expenses list.

All of the above can be considered your basic expenses. Fixed and other basic expenses are necessary, though often you can find opportunities for trimming dollars from your basic expenses, for example, how often you buy cups of Starbuck's coffee or other premium meals or treats.

Next comes your discretionary expenses. Though you can pay for discretionary items with cash or debit cards, a credit card is often used. In this case, reviewing the charges on your credit cards can help you track your discretionary spending. Purchases of clothes, toys, home furnishings, entertainment, and vacation or leisure travel are all examples of discretionary expenses. They are called discretionary because generally you could choose to forego new clothes, a movie, or a new couch, so this expense is created at your discretion.

If you use a credit card for these expenses, review the last twelve months of statements. Jot down the overall amount spent or charged—each month over the year and divide the amount to determine your monthly average spending. If you use more than one credit card for discretionary items, add together all the typical charges to your expenses list. When you decide the final dollar amount to place on your balance sheet, consider first your average spending, then add a further dollar amount to reduce any credit card balance you're carrying. You need to indicate on your expense list a realistic dollar amount that reflects your actual spending habits and a further amount to pay down the credit debt in a reasonable period of time.

What would be a reasonable amount of time? Well, of course, that would depend on how much debt you've accumulated. But for the purposes of getting your arms around your current financial situation, you must know your current level of indebtedness and what it would take, starting today, to eliminate that debt. By the way, if you are putting your gasoline or your groceries or your restaurant meals onto a credit card, stop that immediately. Food and gasoline are basic expenses and should never be purchased on credit. Use a debit card for those items. The only exception to this rule would be in cases where you can and do pay off the credit card balance every month. In that case, simply break out the amount of basic expenses in the monthly bill from the discretionary expenses in the monthly bill.

If you typically use a debit card or cash for purchases like this, which is actually a good thing, do a bit of research to estimate a number that reflects your typical monthly discretionary spending.

Tally both columns. If you're lucky, your income will exceed your expenses. If not, you have to make some changes in order to live within your means.

Running at a Deficit

If your expenses exceed your income, and you are interested in being financially stable or hope to build wealth, you'll have to make some changes. If you don't adjust and become competent in managing your income and finances, you can't proceed to the next level, which is saving money. To save money, you must have money to save. If you're running at a deficit, you simply don't have that money.

I find it amusing when someone tells me that they *are* saving money, despite having a deficit on their balance sheet. They tell me that they are putting away money at work in a 401(k). That's great, but balance sheets do not lie. If you put away $100 a month at work and run at a deficient of $150 month on your balance sheet, are you really saving any money? This is where you have to see that all your finances count. Being financially responsible in one area does not cancel out being remiss in another. You have to manage your whole financial picture.

It's a good thing if you put away that money in a 401(k), which we'll be talking about in another chapter. But this chapter, this rule, is about managing the money you have and living entirely within your means. Without accumulating debt, without requiring bailouts, and without embarrassing overdrafts. The balance sheet is the whole picture.

Credit Is Evil

Credit cards were not part of our household when I was a kid. Back then, people weren't given a credit card unless their income supported prompt repayment. We were on the poor side, so…no credit cards. In more recent years, however, a whole cottage industry has grown up around debt and debtors. The game is to allow people to have credit easily, and then collect unseemly and unending amounts of interest and penalties from hordes of financially hapless people. This game becomes a trap for the targeted rubes—a pool of quicksand, a black hole that many people never escape.

I can vividly remember the first thing I bought on credit. It was a window air conditioner that I got for an apartment in my early twenties. Happily, I was able to pay off that small purchase within a few months. Then things changed. I had established "credit-worthiness." This was when the credit monster came into my life to destroy my personal finances. The offers for credit cards came flooding in. Visa, MasterCard, and nice department stores all offered me a chance to buy clothes and furniture and any number of products whenever I pleased. I admit that having those credit cards and buying those items with those cards gave me a feeling of status. It felt good. The only problem was, of course, that I really couldn't afford those things.

I have been in financial trouble twice in my life, and both times it had to do with credit debt. In those troubled times, those *years* of my life, I was perpetually on the edge of financial ruin. I regularly bounced checks and juggled to pay my bills *every month*, sometimes crazily using credit to do so. I repeatedly moved balances from one card to another, trying to find relief and a lower interest rate, but overall, my debt just grew and grew.

Warning people of the evils of credit debt is like warning people about alcohol usage. You know for a fact that they are going to try drinking, even if you warn them. You also know for a fact that some people can manage drinking without any issue, and that some people are going to become alcoholics and have drinking ruin their lives. Credit debt is like that. It *is* going to take some of you down. Like alcohol, some people can manage credit without any negative effects, and some people will continually suffer over credit issues. Credit debt, particularly for mid-to-lower income types, is extremely destructive.

Some people count on an annual bonus, their tax return, or some other expected windfall, even a someday inheritance, to pay down the build-up of their incurred debt. They run at a negative in their balance sheet for months or years, then use whatever windfall comes to them to pay off or pay down their debt. Then they recommence the debt build-up process again. Of course, this strategy has two problems. One, you risk the chance that whatever windfall you receive is not enough to pay off the debt, and—spoiler alert—it often isn't. Or two, and worse, the windfall might fail to appear.

Other people take on debt knowing they can, and inevitably will, be bailed out of any financial difficulties they get themselves into by a family with financial means. As a strategy for managing your finances, depending on the resources of others generally puts you into the category of a ne'er-do-well. Your family or close friends may come to expect any visit from you as a *"how much do you need?"* encounter. And even within very affluent families, the spigot can be shut off and the errant family member cut off financially.

In still other cases, people simply incur debt with no specific windfall pending or plan for how to pay it off. The accumulation of the debt is often gradual, a chunk here and a few smaller charges there. That was my story of financial woe in my twenties. I had only a vague idea of how my choices, taking on more and more debt, that is, putting charges on credit cards, were impacting my undefined personal balance sheet. Like others, I wanted very much to believe that I could somehow afford the added debt. I was working. I was paying my bills, although just. But I was, obviously, unsophisticated about my finances, since even a basic analysis would have shown that I most certainly couldn't afford that debt.

For some people, easy, widely available credit allows them to have that fancy car, that house or apartment, that nice furniture, those attractive clothes, those swanky vacations, or those pricey gadgets. On another level, easy credit provides lower income people with the means to purchase sometimes desperately needed or, sometimes just desperately desired items – gifts for the kids' birthdays or for the holidays, new clothes for school, a vacation, or technology to stay comparable with other family or peers. In either case, that easy credit puts people's finances at the very limit of and sometimes beyond their actual means. And, over time trains people to live on a hamster wheel of never-ending debt.

It is not uncommon for easy credit to lead to financial trouble. Like me in my twenties, you might be ignoring the math or deluding yourself about what you can really afford. Managing your money means you choose to understand how any specific item of debt will impact your monthly balance sheet. You choose to know when an expense or purchase will eat up all your surplus income or, worse, when it will move you into a monthly deficit. Until you choose to know and manage your personal numbers, you cannot build wealth.

Now, despite the preceding paragraphs and their cautionary words, I'll admit here that some people live quite comfortably in their credit-sponsored world. We'll discuss in a moment the beauty of the middle-class existence that is within reach for most working people today. But by choosing to live just at or beyond your income, you will never accumulate wealth. Debt keeps you working to pay off your past spending and inhibits accumulation of future wealth.

Maybe that's okay with you. In section one, on work, I discussed that people are wired differently about work and money. Some people don't work. Well, here I'll say that some people don't really care to manage their money. They are satisfied if right now they can have all the stuff they want: the gadgets, the car, the house. In exchange, they're okay with not having a big bank account. Even if they crash and burn here or there, have to file bankruptcy, let their house go into foreclosure, give back a car, or endure some other financial calamity, those possibilities do not incentivize such spenders to manage their finances differently.

If questioned about whether they would like to get and stay out of debt and build some personal wealth, they might say yes. But are they willing to do things differently and forgo some of the perks of their current life to achieve that goal? For many, the answer is "no." They like their life, buying all that stuff, and living the seemingly and surprisingly cushy life that credit affords them as a member of our middle class. Before we go further into managing day-to-day finances, let's take a moment to reflect on today's middle-class life.

The Beauty of the Middle Class

Most Americans have no idea how lucky we are to live at a time that has a substantial middle class. Without going too deeply into an anthropological lecture, let's consider the past.

In the early era of the human species, which lasted millions of years, humans existed in small bands or tribes, and their lifestyle was nomadic hunting and gathering. Such societies had, essentially, only a single class. All the members of any given tribe, clan, or band worked cooperatively each day, hunting or gathering, achieving whatever basic subsistence was possible, and all members shared the results. there was little economic differentiation among tribe members. No one had substantially more, and no one had substantially less. If a tribe was poor and starving, all were poor and starving. If the tribe had plenty, all members enjoyed that plenty.

Eventually, human social systems evolved. Once human society began living in stationary settings, a new social paradigm came into existence, that of property ownership, and even more critically, individual property ownership. We entered the era of the "haves" and the "have nots"—or in some cases the "have mores," and the "have lesses."

Once mankind came to see property as something to own and collect, our species began an era where we existed in two distinct classes: the privileged few and the unprivileged masses. It's safe to say that a significant percentage of the human population existed in such a "feudal"-type society for at least thousands of years. Versions of this model existed around the world. In some cases, the ranks of the lower class were indentured, in some cases they were actually slaves, or in some cases they were simply serfs or peasants, that is, poor laborers. In every model, the elite only represented a small percentage of the overall population, and the vast majority of the population were of the poor lower class.

The emergence of a significant third, middle class is more recent. This is not to say that a middle class did not exist at all until recently. No, undoubtedly there were small niches of middle-class populations even in feudal society. Artisans or other specialized workers, servants of the elites, and perhaps ranking warriors may have achieved a higher standard of living than the poor lower classes. By far, though, the largest percentage of the population consisted of the indentured, the landless, the laboring serfs, or peasants.

As denser human population centers expanded, the middle class expanded. During the early centuries of emerging cities, manufacturing, industrialization, and other wage-based work created a growing class of people who were employed and self-supporting unaided by and relatively unbeholden to the elite ruling classes. Furthermore, they were unaffiliated with the indentured or subservient lower classes. These early middle-classers lived quite modestly, however, and could easily slip from the middle-class ranks should misfortune strike their lives.

Starting in the 18th and 19th centuries, skill, knowledge, and education-based employment greatly expanded the ranks of the middle class, and the expansion of those centuries did not compare with the explosion of middle-class employment that occurred in the 20th century. Today, though the middle class is somewhat smaller in third-world countries, most modern countries consist of a dominant middle class. The elite in modern countries, as always, represents only a small but still powerful percentage at the top of the upper classes. Yet, astonishingly, those in what is known as our lower class today, particularly those living at basic subsistence levels, represent only a small percentage. A recent Pew Study on class in the US puts the number of middle-class households at 50%, with approximately equal numbers of lower and upper on either side of the middle-class expanse. And, in true bell-curve fashion, only a very small percentage of our population is represented at the outermost edges of the economic spectrum, which are comprised of the *very* rich or the *very* poor portions of our population.

We are barraged, though, with a disproportionate awareness of the farthest ends of this scale. In particular, we see unending stories and depictions of the rich and famous in our media. Even portrayals of "average people" in television and film often show the characters with fine cars, expensive clothes and electronics, and quite fabulous homes, leading to a belief that average people can and perhaps should have such a lifestyle.

Get Real—Get Happy

What does all this have to do with personal finances? Well, first of all, today's middle-class life, with abundant and inexpensive food, clean water, spacious housing, indoor plumbing, reliable transportation, and a vast assortment of affordable entertainment, represents a kind of life that was undreamt of by the middle class of just a century ago. Some parts of our typical life today would have been lavish for the elite classes of just a few generations past. This level of luxury is readily available and achieved by over 75% of our population. Furthermore, a dreadful lifestyle that involves actual, significant life-threatening health or welfare challenges is, in fact, experienced by only a very small percentage of our population. That small percentage of the grimly stricken or disabled certainly warrants special consideration, but the vast majority of the population has access to unimaginably improved circumstances, in contrast to those humankind has experienced over the ages.

The reason I speak of social classes and the remarkable existence of a dominant middle class is that it *is* a relatively recent phenomenon in human social systems. The current prosperity of our middle class, combined with unprecedented access through media to information about lifestyles and life circumstances has, I think, skewed people's expectations about work and about the lifestyle they might attain or expect through work.

Many people today think that any consistent work must or should lead to significant wealth. They think that because they work, they must be entitled to a new car, to new clothes, to new smartphones, and to the lifestyle they see on television or in social media. After all, the characters they see on television and in film have jobs just like them. I, myself, fell into this trap for a time. On TV, "average" people have amazing clothes, amazing homes, and nice cars and toys. People fail to or choose not to recognize that TV and media lifestyles are not real. People become enthralled by these portrayals, characters, and celebrities, and, having little perspective of how unrealistic and unlikely the depicted lifestyles are, may come to disdain more modest living.

Here's a true story. Joe and Andre, friends of mine, recently retired and bought a nice RV as part of their retirement home-downsizing and life-reorganization, a planned-for and well-thought-out retirement purchase. They invited my spouse and me to a weekend camping excursion. Having pitched a few tents in my low-budget early life, I envisioned a rustic camping scenario. What I saw on this trip amazed me. The "campground" was full of giant RVs and campers, and not just RVs owned by seniors fulfilling a retirement dream. Most were occupied *by families*. There were *hundreds* of giant RVs and giant campers with giant brand-new trucks pulling the campers and countless motorized toys, go-carts, jet-skis, and the like to go along with them. I knew that *I* would certainly be stretched to afford such luxuries, and I am quite well-paid. Is it possible, I thought, that *all these people* make more money than me? And then it hit me. No, *most* of these people probably do not make more money. Instead, more likely, they were just spending extravagantly and were probably deeply in debt with these expensive toys. The future be damned. They were living for today and laying claim to a lifestyle they felt entitled to, with ridiculously over-the-top luxuries, that, in all likelihood, their income did not warrant.

In such a world, it's hard to teach youngsters to appreciate the gift of a comfortable, modest, middle-class life. Instead, parents perpetuate the problem by telling their kids that they can do or have anything. The parents demonstrate this by spending wantonly themselves. The kids, not knowing any better, see their parents' behavior, with cars and homes and lifestyles that are, in reality, beyond their means, or at very least at the outer limit of their means. Then, no surprise, their kids feel entitled to live an over-the-top lifestyle as well.

The truth is that not everyone, and in fact very few, can actually afford such luxuries. Choosing to have them is a trade-off in most cases. And the trade-off is having little to show in savings. In emulating a lifestyle and level of wealth they simply don't have, many of these people are failing to build the actual wealth that might make them financially secure. They live on the brink of financial ruin should there be any disruption in their circumstances or income, and they teach this fiscal irresponsibility to their children. They set up their kids to scorn financial restraint and be dissatisfied with the probable middle-class income they're likely to achieve.

The real truth is that even without all that excessive spending, being middle class in the US is actually pretty darn comfortable. We need to tell kids *that*. We need to talk about how good we all have it. We need to help kids learn that over-the-top spending isn't necessary for happiness, and in most cases is risky. We need to teach the value of restraint, delayed gratification, and financial prudence. And, of course, we need to model that behavior for them. Finally, and critically, we need to remind kids over and over that lifestyles depicted on television and celebrity life depicted in the media are not representative of real life. Real life is different.

We need to talk about careers and working, and the likely lifestyles various career choices will produce. We need to explain how working hard can deliver a good life. *A good life.* A better life than most humans could ever expect, even a few short years ago. If they just work, manage their finances, and live modestly. And, strangely, if they learn the lesson of managing themselves toward a modest middle-class life, that modest behavior can, quite miraculously, often translate into the level of wealth and happiness they might have wished for in their dreams. Our middle-class life has so many benefits, and among those benefits is the freedom to live comfortably *and* to take responsibility for our finances and potentially build wealth.

Managing Finances

Now back to the concept of understanding and managing your finances. As mentioned, some people may not care about managing their finances. They simply allow their financial affairs to happen. They may at times feel flush and comfortable and at other times pinched and financially distressed. If they end up too close to the financial precipice, life events can sometimes push this type of person right off the cliff. You may even know someone who was forced, due to some financial calamity, to file bankruptcy, to have a home or car repossessed, to be evicted, or to require debt consolidation services. Many people regularly bounce checks or have a poor credit score because they can't pay their bills at all or in a timely manner. I have been, as I said earlier, in financial trouble twice in my life, and while I avoided the most severe of the above consequences, I did so only through extreme reorganization of my circumstances. My adjustments included taking second and, briefly, even third jobs, downsizing my living arrangements, selling some of my personal property, and spending *years* reducing my debt and rebuilding my personal finances. Not fun.

It's common for people at some point to find themselves in a financial crisis. In fact, *most* people will face occasional challenges, but in the absence of advance care of their finances, sudden changes will throw some people right over the edge. And when these people face events that impact their finances, I repeat, *as most of us will*, they act surprised. Surprised that they are in a calamity, and surprised and dismayed that they may face negative consequences. Often, they think they're entitled to special breaks, debt forgiveness, or government assistance.

Furthermore, those who have lived high, just at or beyond their means, may suffer greatly in retirement when they no longer have that nice weekly paycheck, or annual bonuses or large tax returns, to bail them out each year—and only a substantially reduced monthly income. They can be forced to spend their last twenty to thirty years in progressively less and less glamorous circumstances, or worse, become another responsibility for their families or our social systems. As a society we are starting to see the widespread impact of the phasing out of secure pensions from average income employment coupled with chronic failure to sufficiently save and exacerbated by rampant excessive spending.

What's the alternative? To manage your finances throughout your life. Make a commitment first to work and maximize your income potential, then to manage whatever income you have to live within your means, and finally, as we will discuss in later chapters, to prepare for your financial future. If you determine that your income is not sufficient to provide you with the lifestyle you believe you are entitled to, you can adjust in only two ways. You can change your income through career transitions, as discussed in the work section, or you can adjust your attitude and spending so that your income covers the financial cost of the lifestyle you can actually afford. These choices are not mutually exclusive. You can work on both. In the last section, we discussed career strategies, and here we will talk about managing your expenses to live within your means.

Let's go through some of your expenses in the three categories: your fixed costs, your basic expenses, and your discretionary expenses. Let's start with fixed costs.

Housing Cost

When creating your personal finance balance sheet, you first added your fixed costs. These are monthly bills that must be paid at a fixed rate. When these expenses are due, you must pay the exact amount owed. Typically, housing is most people's largest single line item. As a rule, your housing cost—your rent or mortgage payment—should not exceed 25-30% of your income. (Less is always good!) No fudging on this. Consider the total monthly income from your job (not before taxes, but your take-home pay), and multiply that amount by 0.30 (30%). This should be your *maximum* total budget for housing. Whatever the amount, compare it to your rent or your mortgage payment. (The mortgage amount should include property taxes, property insurance, and any association fees.) If your housing amount is equal to or less than the budget amount, you are managing housing sensibly.

Some people are "house poor." They've secured an apartment or purchased a home with overhead that exceeds a prudent percentage of their income. In some cases, they may be stuck with an excessive overhead living situation as a result of a failed job, relationship or divorce or even a family inheritance. They might be hoping for a raise or better job or an eventual marriage to make the cost of that housing affordable. Perhaps they take in roommates or stray family members to try to ease the housing cost pain. Or they may jump into co-habiting with a new romantic partner for unromantic, economic reasons. The danger in too-high housing overhead is that you're putting yourself on the edge of your financial capabilities. If you have any blip in your finances, a flakey roommate, a break-up with your boy or girlfriend, or a job loss, you can instantly find yourself in trouble.

I suggest that if your housing cost is higher than 30%, take a long hard look at it. There's no shame in economizing by changing your living situation if you determine that your housing cost is keeping you from financial comfort. At several different points in my life, I have, as already mentioned, downsized and moved into a rented room in one case and a so-called single apartment in another, to regain my financial balance. Give yourself permission to realistically assess your finances and make changes to keep your equilibrium. Even if you don't make a change, *have a plan* to make a change if you need to. Though in more recent years I have been quite financially stable, even within our marriage, my spouse and I have a contingency plan for living in the office/apartment on our property if we ever need to adjust our overhead by renting out or airbnbing our main house.

Here's another great story. Clarisse, a quite successful sales leader, explained that she and her husband recently sold their big Texas house and started renting. Why? Because the property tax on that home was $24,000 annually, not counting the actual mortgage payment! *"Now we can put away thousands of dollars more every month for our last few working years. And we were planning on selling and moving anyway for retirement,"* Clarisse shared.

In today's world, especially using post-Great Recession rationalization, a good number of people are seeking living situations with parents, other family members, or friends, enabling them to live without housing overhead. Be cautious of this tempting option. While living rent-free may take the pressure off you financially, it doesn't really put you into the financially self-supporting category. If you do decide to accept housing from a generous friend or a family member, be a tenant, not a sponge. Pay them rent. Pay it punctually and maintain your self-supporting status. You are not really living as a financially responsible adult until you can manage the cost of maintaining your life. Housing, and being capable of paying for it are, well, basic. Pay them. A reduced amount is acceptable if your purported goal is to save money toward your own place. But you should still pay them rent while setting aside the difference, that is, the dollar amount by which your housing is discounted. After enjoying a lengthy period – or a lifetime – of living rent free, attempting the transition to paying your own way with housing can become a point of failure for the financially challenged.

Renting vs. Purchasing

Another frequently asked question concerns the advisability of renting versus purchasing a home. Another section later in the book explores a home or other real estate purchase as an investment, but here let's simply discuss it from a money-management perspective. As a person who worked in the real estate industry for the past thirty years, you might be surprised to learn that I don't universally support a purchase over a renting option.

For a purchase to make sense, you first have to be quite stable in your employment. This is not to say you need to be making big money. Stability is different. When I worked as a real estate agent, I had one client who was a single administrative assistant and another client who was a gardener. Neither made large sums of money, but in both cases, they had been doing their work for numerous years and had high confidence in the stability of their continued income. Both successfully purchased homes. Another client worked in the television industry, making very good money when she worked. Due to the nature of television employment, her work history and likely future included periods of hiatus every year when her show was not taping, and occasional sudden show cancellations which translated into periods of unemployment. Although this client did purchase a home, her story later involved a foreclosure when she found herself between shows and "upside down," that is, owing more than her home was worth, and unable to sell to get out from under the too-high monthly payment.

The advice I have regarding purchasing a home versus renting comes down first to stability and then to overhead assessment. Assuming a stable income, if you are able to purchase for a dollar amount that compares to the amount you currently already pay, then purchasing is the better option. The upper limit of 30% of your income still applies, of course. The big benefit of purchasing a home is that over time you will be building equity, that is, owning more and more of the home. This can lead to a mortgage-free housing situation in retirement or a tidy lump sum of money for you to cash out at some later point. Long term, this generally works. In some cases, you may also be eligible for an annual tax deduction for the interest you pay on your loan.

Going into a home purchase that will dramatically change your overhead, however—for example, from living with your parents rent-free or for a nominal rent to a significant monthly mortgage payment—can be a serious challenge for many first-time buyers. Prior to the Great Recession, the pressure was to buy at any cost and to purchase the most expensive house you might qualify for. Mortgage companies had played their part in this irresponsible game by creating a wide assortment of mortgage types, often with low entry teaser rates. The low entry rates allowed the purchase of bigger, more expensive homes, but also required higher payments in later years. The thinking was that over time your improving income would make the larger payment feasible. And, they promised, the value of the property would go up, making that stretch home purchase a financially sound investment. The problems came when values didn't keep going up, and actually fell dramatically. Then, when unemployment also rose during the Great Recession, it became clear that this "buy as much house as you possibly can" strategy *was not* financially sound. The outcome was record numbers of foreclosures and countless Americans with devastated personal finances.

Again, my advice is to purchase a home only if the monthly payment is comparable to the amount you already pay in rent and aligned with the 30% of *net* income mentioned previously. Know, too, that the "payment" should include taxes and insurance, and if applicable, associations fees, not just the mortgage itself. Don't let a mortgage loan officer or real estate agent convince you differently. I certainly have not always been wildly savvy with finances, but when it came to my first home purchase, I balked at the hefty amount my lender said I qualified for. Instead, I bought a home for about half that amount and took on a payment that was only a few hundred dollars more than my modest rent at the time. Because of that single prudent decision, I have never had trouble covering the mortgage payment, even during lean times. The home, which I now share with my spouse, is small. But the reasonableness of our housing cost still gives me comfort.

Having worked in the real estate industry for much of my career I certainly am an advocate of the benefits of home ownership. But there is no shame in renting. I came from an upbringing were my family rented. And yes, I saw some of the downside of renting, such as a landlord who was slow to do any repairs, and unexpected and exorbitant raises in rents. But homeownership has challenges too. When a roof leaks or a pipe bursts, well, guess what? That's your job to fix. And, while it was great fun painting all the rooms in my house when I first moved in, the nth time those walls need painting, or that carpet needs to be replaced, or the bathroom requires updating, well, you get the idea. At some point you can understand why our old landlord looked so weary every time my mom called him to repair something that was broken.

Furthermore, extracting yourself from a too-high mortgage if your circumstances change is much more complex than just giving up a rented apartment or house. In some cases, the consequences can be significant. Just ask anyone who ended up in a foreclosure situation or short-sell scenario. The real lesson, whether in a renting situation or a home purchase, is to keep your housing overhead manageable.

Automobile Cost
Most people's second highest monthly fixed cost is their automobile expense, including car payment and insurance. If you are living without a car or a car payment, good for you. If you do not utilize a car at all, using public

transportation or car services instead, you can skip the next couple of paragraphs.

Car expense should not take more than 10-15% of your net income. Same deal here as with housing. Multiply your net income by 0.15, and that is your maximum auto budget (less is always better).

True story. I briefly dated someone who drove a very cool convertible BMW sports car but found out on our second date that this person still lived with her parents. The car payment and insurance were so high, that, though she worked at a steady, full-time job, she could not afford to pay rent. Instead, she was living in a spare bedroom at her parents' home. That is called "car poor." For some, the attraction of the fancy car, and the inexplicable availability of credit to allow such an imprudent financial choice, make the irrational car purchase irresistible. By the way, did I date that person for long? No. This wasn't a fiscally responsible adult, and by that point in my life I knew better than to become entangled with someone whose priorities include an expensive, fancy car instead of rent.

If you own your car outright, and currently do not have a car payment, be aware that cars don't last forever. Look at a car payment as a fixed cost. For the time you own your current car outright, set aside the dollar amount of that absent monthly payment to save for *the next* car. Yes, that's right. Prepare for when you will need your next car, because you can be sure you will eventually be faced with the "crisis" of your car breaking down or needing prohibitively priced repairs.

Purchase or Lease?

This is another common question. Here again I want to point out that car dealers often push car leases for people with no business having a lease. In reality, car leases have a very narrow range of appropriate users. Leases work great in situations where someone is not particularly hard on a vehicle, does not put an excessive number of miles on it, and would, in any case, update their vehicle every few years. Often this is a sensible move for a prestige-minded person with plenty of money. I have also heard of retirees who like the idea of regular replacement vehicles, and lower payments, accepting that using a car lease places automotive cost perpetually on their balance sheet. The lower payment for the lease reflects the fact that you're not really buying the car. You're renting it. That's why it's called a lease.

Too often people go for a lease because the lease is *the only way* they can afford a particular car's payment. That's a problem in two ways. First, it reflects the ongoing issue of trying to portray yourself living at an income level you don't possess. And second, taking on a lease on a vehicle you can't otherwise afford means you're very unlikely to be able to afford to buy out the lease at the end of the lease term. And because you're leasing the car just to keep a lower payment, you may not be the type of owner who conforms to the many strict lease provisions, such as the limits on mileage or maintaining the condition of the vehicle to required standards. When the lease term ends, unpleasant financial consequences can follow. Without the cash to buy out the lease, you may be forced into another lease, sometimes with worse terms due to penalties, putting yourself in another unnecessary debt loop. And in this payment loop, you will not even have ownership at the end.

Many people struggle with automotive debt. This is a cycle you can break. Choose to see your transportation costs within the context of your income and budget, instead of viewing your car through the lens of a lifestyle you wish you could afford. I still smile when I think about the first and few subsequent dates I had sitting in that sporty little BMW. I knew then and know now that such a car is not a responsible vehicle for an average worker.

Dating and Managing Money

Speaking of dating, remember how you're not going to date anyone who isn't working? Well, take heed of reckless or overspending, too. If your prospective partner is working, even at a relatively good job, but seems to be emulating a lifestyle of the rich and famous, well, again, I say take heed. *Before* you fall in love, take note if they have a home or apartment that is crazily posh, an excessively luxurious car, stupidly expensive clothes, a flashy new phone and other pricey gadgets, and/or are wantonly spending on food, partying, or entertainment. Don't be naive and assume they are rich. Ask. You can do this playfully, but it is reasonable to determine if this person you are dating is truly wealthy and can, indeed, afford all the goodies. Or if they're just an average worker and are spending recklessly.

I have dated both types. I dated someone who had a bigger annual income from her trust account than I was likely to make in my lifetime. And I've dated people who constantly juggled bills to keep up the appearance of a chic lifestyle.

Once you know what you are dealing with, ask yourself if this person's style of money management is going to lead to a secure future for you and any kids you may have. Big spenders might be fun to date and can give you some great memories, but they might not provide you with a happy, financially sound ever-after. In relationships I firmly advise—*no victims*. If you proceed with someone who is clearly showing they are a "live-for-today" person or irresponsible with their money— "oh, yeah, I filed bankruptcy…." "Well, you know, my credit got slammed when I was laid off…."—you cannot later cry about the fact that together the two of you have not saved enough for your retirement. Before you fall in love and can't think of living without this person, assess if they are a strong financial partner. If not, before you fall in love, move on.

Other Fixed Expenses

To finish up the section on your fixed expenses, let's consider student loan debt or child support payments if you have these obligations. Unfortunately, you are unlikely to be able to economize on either of these expenses, as the terms are generally firmly set, in some cases by a court. Furthermore, as a strong advocate for personal responsibility in your financial obligations, I cannot support defaults or deadbeats. If you are truly struggling to meet your obligations, you can try to pursue exculpation or a restructure of the debt. And, court mandates for fixed child support payments can be challenged if your circumstances have changed. If you do choose to pursue adjustments along these lines, don't go into default in advance of the appeal.

Basic Expenses

Next, consider the basic expenses that aren't fixed, but go up or down due to numerous factors. First are utility bills. Replacing the former world of home telephone bills is mobile phone service. While having some type of cellular service is a standard utility cost today, the cost for such service can vary significantly. I personally cut my monthly mobile phone cost in half with a simple assessment of my phone usage and changing a few data settings, and by attentive usage of free WiFi.

Other utility costs may seem fixed, but behavior has lots to do with these bills. Air conditioning often leads to high utility costs during summer months but is actually a manageable expense. No one dies from having a thermostat set at 78 or even 80 degrees. The entire world lived without air conditioning for millions of years. You *can* stand being a bit warm during the summer. Your parents were not crazy misers when they chided you to keep the door closed or turn off the lights. During colder months you can add a sweater or extra blanket rather than cranking up the thermostat. Today, there are numerous ways you can economize in your utility payments.

Beyond utility expenses are your other basic expenses, including food and essential supplies for living. I think most people know that money spent on food can vary dramatically from person to person. For example, buying breakfast at Starbucks, just coffee and a bagel, will cost you between $7 and $10 per day. If you do this even four days a week, that puts your breakfast at about $1,500 per year. Making a cappuccino at home using a $60 machine and making oatmeal or buying a bag of bagels can cut the cost of breakfast by 70%. That translates to over a thousand bucks in your pocket! Eating out for lunch every day at work might be fun, but it is also a cost. $10-$15 dollars a day, four days a week—that is over $2500 a year. Dinner is a whole other world of cost. The average dinner in a low-to-mid range restaurant is about $50 for two, with drinks, tax, and tip. Eating out three times per week? Over $7,000 annually. Go to the market. If you cannot cook, buy frozen meals or visit the deli and purchase pre-made lunch and dinner options.

You don't have to stop eating out altogether. Just be aware of how much you are spending and reduce. One trick is to never use a credit card for eating out. Only use cash or a debit card. Or try tracking your eating out expenditures and then reducing the total month over month. Remember that managing finances is all about knowing about and taking responsibility for your spending. By being attentive to your spending, you can choose to cut your basic expenses dramatically.

Discretionary Expenses

Finally, we have discretionary expenses. I recall a family member of mine who has struggled with her finances over the years once explaining that she had just bought a new dining room set that they "really needed." I know people with modest incomes who regularly book trips to exotic locales. We all, at some point, or in some areas, purchase items that are, in reality, not needed. The only questions I have about these optional purchases are whether they create on-going debt or potentially diminishing the spenders' future security?

Credit cards and debt are, as I mentioned, the greatest source of financial calamities. If your budget is already tight, or you are accumulating debt, additional significant, non-essential purchases might be better postponed. If you are debt-free, that is another matter. I repeat that some people spend everything they make, and financial prudence is not high on their list. Even if you are careful to stay within the lines of managing to the limits of your income, debt can be the straw that breaks your financial back.

Another point, and this ties into later sections on savings, is that credit debt is rarely offered for free. Usually, you are charged interest for the privilege of spending money now that you do not have and paying off that spending over time. Credit card interest, even at a good, low rate, will most often be over 10%. Perhaps you currently have a savings account. What interest rate are you *collecting* on those dollars? It doesn't take a rocket scientist to see that $5,000 in debt carried at 10% interest is costing you far more than $5,000 in savings is earning you at 1.5%. After this part of my talk, people ask me, "Should I pay off my credit card debt with my savings?" The answer is yes only if you can refrain from running the debt up again. The debt is the problem. The solution is to live within your means.

A good book to read that covers some similar ground is *Set for Life* by Scott Trench. I don't agree with everything Trench suggests, but you can't argue with his frugal-living suggestions.

Off the Cliff: Financial Crisis

When you find yourself in a bad way financially, it's tempting to look for any way out. The preferred path is always the path of working through the crisis yourself, that is, to manage your current situation to get your financial footing back or dig yourself out of whatever hole you are in—

[118]

however slowly, however long it takes. If you've lost your job, get a temporary job. If you still have your job, get a second job or work extra hours. Sell off your personal property. Cancel your cable subscription or otherwise lower your overhead. Managing through a crisis is always preferable, because you're owning your financial problems and taking responsibility for fixing them.

I'm always disappointed when I hear unhappy stories among my acquaintances of the devastating impact of unexpected job loss, or of being hit with a significant unanticipated expense, or even when I hear laments over run-away debt accumulation. When a crisis occurs, it's true that getting your finances back in order is painful. I've been through it. But here's a fact. Most of us will have unexpected financial challenges. Living very close to the financial edge, failing to set aside an emergency fund, or racking up crushing debt just makes these common life trials more impactful.

But, regardless of the root cause, sometimes there *is* a significant crisis. What then?

— *Tapping Home Equity*
Some people treat their home like an ATM machine. With every economic boon, they see the equity in their home like money that is available to spend. So, let's talk about this. One of the differences between renting and buying your housing is that buying potentially offers you ownership. Initially when you purchase, you actually own very little of your home.

The bank owns most of it. Over the years, though, as you pay your mortgage, you slowly own more and more of your home. The amount of the home you own is called your equity. If the real estate market is good, you can further increase equity based on the increased market value of the home. The goal is to eventually own the home outright and potentially eliminate housing cost in your retirement years. Or, as an alternative, to reap the equity cash when you sell the home and use it either to offset the purchase cost of your next home or bolster your retirement funds.

If, before one of the happy final outcomes above occurs, you find yourself in a financial crisis or have accumulated overwhelming debt, should you tap this equity? In fact, having a home worth significantly more than you currently owe on the mortgage makes the equity a common target for the financially strapped. But is that equity the best source for your bailout funds? Well, a cash-out refinance *can* be one answer.

Of course, a refinance resets the thirty-year term of your loan, and depending on your age, may preclude you from ever reaching that mortgage-free retirement goal. In some cases, you can preserve your current monthly payment amount, and occasionally even reduce it, depending on interest rates and the amount of equity you have.

If you pursue this option, be sure that whatever cash you take out *is* used smartly to alleviate the crisis or eliminate your debt. Having to tap your mortgage to fix your financial problems is nothing to brag about. It is, however, one way you can bail yourself out of a financial hole using your own means. I did it myself during my second bout with financial difficulties. But remember that with every bailout the trick is to use the money wisely and avoid another financial crisis down the line.

Here's another true story. When a serious and expensive home repair was required, Jane and Dominick didn't have the necessary savings available to do the needed work. So, they decided to tap their home equity, pushing back their loan of ten years, and resetting the 30-year timeline. While discussing the refinance, Jane shared that Dominick's old car would soon need to be replaced. In addition to repairing their home, and as a reasonable part of the refinance plan, Jane and Dominick decided to pull out enough cash to purchase a modest car replacement for Dominick.

Listening to this plan, I thought it was unfortunate that they had to use that equity, but it was nevertheless a rational plan. Months later, when discussing the process, Jane sheepishly admitted that she and her husband had ultimately used the dollars allocated to the car purchase as a down payment on a new car and had taken on a car payment. Jane justified the decision saying Dominick *deserved* a nice, brand-new vehicle because he worked hard. I just had to shake my head. This couple, who did not have the savings needed to pay for an emergency home repair, had decided that a new car payment was somehow comfortably within their budget.

— *Tapping Retirement Accounts*
What about tapping a retirement account to pay off debt? All I can say here is that I recommend doing everything possible to avoid raiding your retirement account(s) to cover a financial crisis or pay off debt. As mentioned above, it might feel good to use your own funds to manage through a crisis or pay off your debt. Do what you need to do. But in the coming chapters, we will revisit the importance of having and protecting your future financial security as the next rule of personal finances. If you are currently deeply upside down on your income-to-debt balance sheet, you need to fix *that* before you can responsibly move to higher-level financial management. So, again, do what you need to do, and then make a commitment to learn the crux of this lesson, which is to manage your finances to live within your current means.

– *Taking Out a Loan*

Taking out a loan to get through a crisis or to fix debt problems is an extremely risky business. Whether you get the loan from a family member, use available credit, or go to a debt-consolidation organization, the danger is, of course, that you have the good intention of paying off the new loan, but don't yet have the financial resources or discipline to follow through. You might indeed *want* to get back on your feet financially or to stop reckless debt accumulation, but the loan is often just a temporary band aid that makes it possible to not make painful and needed changes. As with every remedy in this section, the final statement is: do what you feel you need to do but know that you will probably need to change your lifestyle. Take ownership of the root cause of those financial problems and be sure you do not repeat the problem.

– *Payday Loans*

Payday loans are a short-term fix for an immediate financial pinch, and payday loan companies have become omnipresent, particularly in lower economic areas. The interest rates charged for this type of bridge loan are high, much higher than any conventional loan. Terms are easy, though, and money is produced instantly. Users of these loans rationalize that the overall dollar amount paid in interest will not be substantial, because you pay the loan off when you get your paycheck. But needing to use this type of loan to tide you to your next paycheck is symptomatic of an underlying money mismanagement issue. The answer, as in all areas of this rule, is to learn to manage your money to live within your means, without requiring the services of a pricey emergency-loan agency.

— *Knee-Breakers*
Some people in financial distress accept loans from disreputable and even illicit money lenders. While a payday loan company might take unseemly interest from you, they are nevertheless a legal business. Sometimes, your distress and desperation may make you a target for "offers" from the darker side of lending. Taking such money to bale yourself out of a financial hole rarely ends well and can place you in a deeper and darker hole than you ever imagined.

— *Bankruptcy*
If you were hoping that this final section was going to give you permission to file bankruptcy because you want to start fresh and do better, then you're reading the wrong book. Laws in the US that allow debtors to write off their debt are, in my opinion, much too liberal. I know more than a few people who have filed

for bankruptcy more than once. Taking on a debt and then not paying the debt was once considered a crime. Today people act like they are just unfortunate victims of circumstance. I believe part of the blame lies with the credit or lending institutions that continue to offer credit or loans to abusers and bumpkins and then pass the cost of that risky behavior to the rest of us. But regardless, I am an advocate for personal responsibility.

So there. One last time let me reiterate, if you are in a crisis or owe lots of money, get a second job or a third. Sell your jewelry, car, or other goodies you may have bought. Sell your house and downsize your living situation. And, most importantly, stop the behavior that has led you to be in the financial crisis.

— *Windfall Money*
On a happier note, most people will have one or more events in their life that result in windfall money, that is, money not earned as a wage, but that comes to you through life events, such as an inheritance or some sort of legal settlement. I once received a pretty substantial separation check after an organizational layoff, and I have known couples who received considerable dollars in "gift money" at their wedding. There are also more regular windfall money events, like annual bonuses or surprisingly large tax returns.

Given that most people will at least occasionally have a windfall, let's consider how you might choose to handle your windfall dollars. Maybe you know of a case where a friend or family member used an unexpected windfall to purchase a fancy new car, a motorcycle, a boat, a dream vacation, or even cosmetic surgery. I've actually heard the words, "My mom would want me to take this vacation." These people reason that they will never have this kind of cash again, and therefore should "live large" on the windfall. They are, of course, probably correct. They probably won't ever have that kind of cash again— because prudently managing their money does not seem to be on their list of things to do.

As mentioned earlier, there is also the situation where paying off existing debt seems the only sensible course with windfall money. Paying down or paying off debt seems a grudgingly responsible allocation of windfall money. Let me say here that paying off debt would be supremely worthwhile if no recurrence of the indebtedness followed, but in many cases, staying debt-free may not follow.

I've also seen cases of placing the windfall into a savings account with every good intention of retaining it. Those good intentions are followed by a slow chipping away of the dollars when monthly expenses or small discretionary expenditures come up.

How you handle windfall money often reflects your truest financial character. From the "throwing it out the window" exuberance, to the debt/payoff/debt cycle, to the slow seepage of funds from between your fingers. Most often, people handle windfall cash in alignment with their overall financial patterns. This is why people who receive even a significant windfall, like a lottery win, often over the long-term return to their original financial situation.

What then, you might ask, is recommended? You might be surprised to read my advice, which starts with knowing yourself. If you currently have no savings or money in investments to speak of, and currently spend every bit of your income, you are unlikely to meaningfully embark on a path of wealth accumulation with your windfall. You might as well continue in your pattern. Take that trip. Buy that Harley. If your pattern involves racking up debt then paying it down with windfall money, then do what you do.

On the other hand, I do not advise putting your windfall money into an easy-access account and tapping it here and there for day-to-day expenses. When you slowly erode that windfall money—which, incidentally, I did with that large separation check I received after being a laid off—you will end up with nothing to show for it, not even a great memory from a dream vacation. Using windfall dollars as a financial cushion for your day-to-day living expenses also hinders you from learning the lesson of living within your actual income.

Of course, you *can* do something different. If you are choosing to truly embrace this rule, you can use a windfall to mark the starting point for a new financial approach. You can "manage" that money. That is, you can make a clear plan for it. It's okay to use a portion of windfall money to purchase something fun, but it's irresponsible to "blow" all of it. It's okay, in fact a great idea, to pay down debt, but you must then commit to refraining from again running your debt up. If you're ready to take the step to responsibly manage your windfall money, here's my formula for allocating those rare extra dollars.

— *Windfall Money Rule of Thirds*
First, let me present my windfall situation. Because my family was poor, I have never received any inheritance. I am not and hope never to be litigious, so no legal settlements. In my employment situation, however, I do get annual bonuses. And in past years, as mentioned, I had separation agreements and sizable checks from my soon-to-be former employers. So, that about accounts for all my windfall money.

Here's my strategy. I call it the rule of thirds. Life's too short to deny yourself any fun at all with windfall money. I allocate a third of my windfall money to fun—a vacation or a frivolous purchase. In past years, my spouse and I have taken nice vacations, and one year we bought a little cabin in the mountains, which we see as a fun getaway spot, but which also has some limited investment value.

I allocate another third of my windfall money to strict savings. That is, I move a portion of the windfall money into a no-touch account, a CD or other account that's not easily accessed. We'll explain more about CDs and other savings options in the next section. In some years, we have used a bit of the "savings" dollars to buy small amounts of individual stocks, and we maintain a very modest stock investment portfolio. We'll will explore the subject of investing in stocks in the investing section.

The last third of my windfall money is allocated to prudent spending. The first and obvious example of prudent spending is to pay down or pay off any debt. Other examples of prudent spending include pricey but non-emergency repairs or updates to our home, furniture, electronics, or automotive repairs or replacement. I'm not a frivolous car purchaser, so whatever vehicle we, as a couple, decide to purchase is made as a practical decision, not as a woohoo thrill. Home repairs are an endless drain, and in homeownership many couples struggle to keep up their property. We keep an on-going list of needed updates or repairs, plus other upgrades or replacements we would like, and we try to take care of one or more every year. We're close to retirement, so we recognize that when the annual bonuses stop, finding money for such repairs or updates will be more challenging. So, we're trying to prepare as best we can for the looming retirement years and subsequent budget constraints.

The rule of thirds is not a hard-and-fast rule. Your percentage of allocations may vary. Maybe you will have a rule of fourths rather than thirds and have another category. Maybe, particularly if the windfall amount is large, you may want to put more into savings to grow your wealth. Or, if you receive regular, annual windfall dollars, as I do with bonuses, you can adjust on a year-to-year basis. For us, there were years we allocated almost all the windfall dollars to one purchase, for example, the year we bought the cabin, and last year when I purchased a slightly used car. In those years, only a small dollar amount went into the no-touch savings bucket, and trips to the cabin had to suffice as our vacation.

The real point when a windfall comes is to have a plan for the dollars and manage it. In some cases, such as with an inheritance or a litigation settlement, you may never again have another jackpot like that. Convince yourself that it doesn't matter and blow it or convince yourself that the windfall can be the start of a new financial future for you. In either case, you'll probably be right.

Your Money Management Report Card: FICO Scores

These days, everyone gets a report card on their financial management. It's called your FICO score, also known as your credit score or rating. This score is used as an overall indication of how you manage your money in terms of debt and paying your bills. All formal debt is reported to credit agencies and your FICO score (the name originating from Fair Isaac Credit Company) is based on the three large credit information bureaus' reports. If you pay your bills on time, it's reported. If you're late in paying bills, that's reported too. If you default on any debt, yep, that will be reported and become a black mark on your credit history. Bankruptcies, foreclosures, evictions, repossessions, and bounced checks are all similarly reported. Your score goes up when you manage your finances well, pay your bills on time, and keep your debt down. Your score tanks when you have issues. Some people shrug about their poor FICO score and just accept the consequences. Someone told me recently that they were forced to take an automobile loan at 18% interest because of their poor credit. Ugh!

If you want a better score, all you have to do is manage your finances as we have suggested. Live within your means. You don't need high income to have a high credit score. The score is computed on your performance, not on your income. FICO scores do not speak to overall wealth or future security either. They're only a measure of how well you manage your money. You can, theoretically, have a great credit score, be great at day-to-day financial management, and still end up with few financial resources in retirement. This leads to our next section where we take your financial education into the realm of the building security for your future.

Rule Three: Save

Retire? I'd love to, but I can't afford to retire.
-a 72-year-old acquaintance of mine

Compound interest is the eighth wonder of the world.
-Albert Einstein

Finances for Your Future

This next rule, the Save rule, marks a crossing point. The first two rules are about taking day-to-day financial responsibility for yourself. You work. You manage your finances. When you begin to save and invest, you're taking long-term financial responsibility for yourself and can, theoretically, begin building wealth.

For the purposes of this book, we define wealth as "an ample supply of money." What, you might ask, constitutes an ample supply? It's an amount that ensures your ability to maintain a quality of life, or lifestyle, that's desirable for you throughout the years you're alive, through the ups and downs of life, and, in some cases, throughout the years of your spouse's and potentially your children's lives as well.

Now, this may not sound very glamorous as a goal. Feel free to aspire to greater wealth than defined here. The principles outlined in the book will hold true for any level of wealth you aspire to attain. But as I presented in the introduction to this book, I assume nothing. Most people *do not* have the wealth I refer to above. They have not collected a sufficient supply of money to ensure a desirable lifestyle throughout their life, and in some cases can't even ensure their lifestyle through economic blips.

Perhaps, as we discussed in rule two, you are able to maintain a fine living standard now, while you are working. That's great. It *is* admirable. Not everyone can make such a claim. But now consider the future. Even if you *want* to continue to work forever, you may not be *able* to work forever. Your body or health may make the decision for you. Social advancement or progress may make the decision for you. Economic or historical events may make the decision for you. You could experience a personal catastrophe, such as a heart attack, cancer, or stroke, a company layoff, a natural disaster, or other event (even a pandemic) that disrupts or ends your current income. And of course, many of us do *want* to simply retire, to have time for other activities and goals. Aging is a fact of life. The alternative is death, so I think most of us would choose the aging option. Yet, not having financial resources to tide you through an income disruption or to ensure a comfortable retirement is all too common.

No matter your age now, think about it. If you experienced a major income disruption right now, how would you fare? Would you be able to maintain your current lifestyle? And for how long? Would such an event require you to raid your retirement savings? Do you have a contingency fund? Do you have a conservation plan?

How about your retirement? Do you have a vision of what your lifestyle will look like in retirement? Are you still living in your cushy house? Are you still driving a nice car, upgraded every few years? Do you see yourself traveling? Do you see yourself golfing, going to concerts or sporting events, or doing other fun activities? Or do you see yourself living in your daughter's basement bedroom, with her husband and kids living up above? Do you see yourself without a car or with a dilapidated one because you can't afford payments? Do you see yourself having your breakfast or dinner "out" at the local McDonald's? And, what if you don't have kids that you can live with? Do you see yourself living in a rented room somewhere? While I don't consider the latter possibilities to be horrible options, they may not be the retirement of your dreams.

You have to ask yourself, what will you do when you retire from working, when, through your own choice or life events, you are no longer gainfully employed? What does your financial position look like at that point? Will you be financially secure? You'll have social security, eventually, yes. But social security provides only the lowest level of financial support for people's retirement, even less than the national poverty level. Social security is only designed to keep you from starving, not to provide you will a nice retirement. Some of you may be, or will be, vested in a pension. That's good. Consider the projected dollar amount of that pension and add it to the savings and social security. Will it be enough to live comfortably?

What else will you have? Savings? As a rough estimate, look at your current total savings and then divide that amount by 30, and then by 12, and you'll see how much or little you'll have to supplement your monthly income for the average retirement planning span of thirty years. We'll look more deeply into financial planning in the conclusion of this book, but for now let's consider that successful personal finances must involve more than just working and managing your finances day-to-day.

Making money, that is working, and managing your money responsibly *are* the essential first rules in being financially successful in life. But for financial *security* you have to do more. You have to consider the future. So, the next two rules focus on building or accruing wealth. Underlying these rules is a critical lesson, the lesson of having money and not spending it. Many people simply can't "get" this lesson and therefore fail to accrue any substantial wealth.

Generally, there are two avenues for building personal wealth: saving and investing. Rules three and four focus on saving and investing, respectively. Some people struggle with the distinction between saving and investing. Since both saving and investing can translate into growing your overall wealth, it's worth a few lines of definition here.

The primary difference between saving and investing is risk. With saving you have no risk to your principal, which is the amount of money you start with or add as you go. As a note, there's technically a very small risk even with saving. For example, it's possible for a bank to collapse, or for saved dollars to be embezzled or robbed, but such occurrences are unusual and not inherent in the nature of saving.

Saving *can* produce a return, however. In other words, saving can produce *additional* money to add to the principal. But the main characteristic of saving is that dollars placed into savings will never incur a loss of your initial amount, that is, your principal. Money held as savings can have an ROI (return on investment) which can go up or down, based on market conditions or your choices, but the ROI cannot become negative. The return from saving can be, and often is, quite a small amount or even zero, as we will demonstrate. But the nature of saving is that the principal is always preserved.

Investing, on the other hand, *always* involves some level of risk. Even safer investments such as mutual funds involve risk. In investment situations, the ROI can go up or down, as with savings ROI, but, importantly, with investing the ROI can *and does* go into negative numbers on occasion. In this case you can lose some or in extreme cases all of the original investment dollars. We talk about investing in the next section.

I'm amused by how different people react to this part of their financial education. For some people, the minute I speak about the possibility of a negative impact to the principal, they're, like, *"No way man. None of that investing for me. No risk. Not my game. I am a savings person all the way."*

Others when we cover the same material hear me speak of small to no returns, and they're, like, *"No, way man. I'm in it to win it. I'll take the risk and show you the glory of large returns."* We'll discuss risk more in both this and the next section.

Not All Savings Are Equal

Savings (the noun) refers to dollars that are set aside, not to be used for day-to-day living. If you simply leave extra dollars in your bank account as a cushion for day-to-day expenses, it's hard to call those extra dollars savings. To have savings, there should be a clear differentiation between those and the dollars you might use to live on. Therefore, saving (the verb or action) generally involves putting the dollars in a designated place. Importantly, having your savings in a separate place allows you to know the amount of savings you have. This relates back to the rule about managing and tracking your finances. Now let's consider places you can put your savings and the pros and cons of each.

Mattress Money

Strange as it is to say, even in today's world, some people still like the idea of keeping their money close. They like seeing and touching their dollars. Beyond the gratification of holding, counting, and playing with a bunch of money—and I do see the fun in it—this is not the best saving strategy. It's perfectly reasonable to keep a reserve of cash on hand, for example, in case of a natural disaster that might temporarily take down electronic capabilities. I live in earthquake country and I keep a few hundred dollars in cash in my home for such a possibility. But beyond that, you might be edging toward institutional paranoia, "prepper" territory, or apocalyptic thinking.

If some of your money comes from undocumented sources, such as under-the-table work or sales you don't report, you may think it prudent to keep your surplus earnings in an undocumented location. Funds significantly beyond your reported means can raise a red flag with authorities. This is a common dilemma for criminals, that is, where to stash all their ill-gotten dollars. Hence home safes and hidey-holes.

In any case, the biggest, typically cited downside to mattress money in terms of wealth-building is that mattress money has zero ROI (return on investment). Though you'll have your money, it won't generate any return or added money for you. A possible worse downside is that, no matter how discreet you try to be, you could become known as a person who has substantial cash money on hand and therefore become a target. As an older person, you're particularly vulnerable. Even if you keep your cash in a well-hidden safe, you can still be burgled or robbed. And it's very hard for a cash hoarder to keep that fact a secret, since most of us have family or close friends who will inevitably become privy to your saving strategy. Oh yes, I've heard the tough talk, "Let them just try…," but wealth building is a long game, and homes will be left unattended for periods of time. I simply suggest that this is not the best strategy.

Though more secure, placing cash dollars in a safety deposit box is still technically a mattress-money option. That money is earning nothing for you. In a safety deposit box, it won't even serve as emergency money in case of a natural disaster, since banked funds, particularly funds that are not documented in accounts, may be inaccessible during a crisis.

Extra Dollars in Your Checking Account

In general, as already mentioned, leaving extra dollars in your checking account does not really constitute saving. This is partly because at any point you can, and likely will, draw on those funds to manage the ups and downs of your day-to-day finances. And, rest assured, there will be ups and downs. Besides, as also mentioned, it's very difficult to calculate your savings when your funds are co-mingled with the dollars marked for living expenses.

Furthermore, most checking accounts offer little to no interest. Even checking accounts that do purportedly offer interest will offer extremely low rates. While some interest is better than none, as in the mattress-money strategy, often the ROI on an interest checking account won't even keep up with inflation, which we'll discuss later.

A Savings Account Linked to Your Checking Account

This is better. Savings linked to your checking offers the benefit of separate accounting. While the proximity to your checking account and ease of use may seem like a benefit, this is actually a drawback. The intention with saving is to accumulate wealth, so easy access allows the financially undisciplined to easily tap into and deplete the savings. A benefit, however, of any traditional savings account is that interest will be offered, though the typical interest rate at a local bank or credit union is usually quite low compared to other saving options.

The best and most sensible use of a savings account in your local bank or credit union is to maintain a prudent reserve or emergency fund. A prudent reserve is an amount of savings that equals one or two months of expenses, and is readily accessible in case of emergency, or that acts as a hedge against an overdraft in your checking account—though the better you get at the managing your finances the more infrequent this should be. Common examples of such emergencies include injuries that take you out of work for a time, being unexpectedly let go from your current job, having a surprise personal, home, or car expense, or more rarely a natural disaster or economic crisis. I wrote parts of this book in the Spring of 2020, a time of an unprecedented national health crisis and sudden interruptions of income for millions of Americans. Sadly, many—too many—Americans didn't have sufficient reserves to bridge even a few months of income interruption.

As an example, Sally, a social acquaintance, lamented that she and her husband had launched a new athletic training business just before the COVID-19 shut-down. After several months of closure, she admitted that she and her husband had used all their remaining savings and raided their retirement accounts to stay afloat. Sally shared that she was now considering applying for a job with her former employer. Of course, I felt awful for her and her husband. This couple had put most of their financial chips on the table to pursue the dream of small business ownership, and then the unexpected shut-down hammered their nascent business. My only mental comment was that they might have saved some of their retirement nest egg had they accepted the need to get back into paid employment a bit sooner, even as a temporary measure.

The beauty of having a robust reserve is that you can handle a financial gap without running up your credit debt, suffering credit damage, or raiding your retirement funds. The reserve keeps you afloat, short term, should you need to transition work-wise, retrench your living arrangements, put out a substantial dollar amount for a purchase or repair, or just to plain live on during a crisis. As mentioned, the amount of this reserve should equal several months of living expenses and should be maintained at all times. Once used, you should strive to replenish your reserve immediately, particularly if you've tapped it for an unexpected expense or an overdraft. If you're disciplined enough to maintain this type of reserve, then you may establish other savings elsewhere, as this reserve money has been earmarked specifically for unexpected events.

Earmarked Savings

Since we just defined a prudent reserve as an earmarked savings fund, let's explore the concept of earmarked funds or savings further. I'm a big believer in earmarking funds. In life, there are important big-ticket events or purchases that will require substantial dollars. I'm surprised how often people choose to put these easily foreseeable big-ticket items onto credit that then create many months or years of debt.

A better strategy is to create and begin funding earmarked accounts—one for the next new car, one for the annual vacation, one for holiday spending, one for your son's or daughter's wedding, one as a college fund for your kid(s), one for a down payment on a house. You get the idea. This can be done quite easily. Today, many savings institutions allow for weekly, bi-weekly, or monthly automatic transfers to be pulled from your checking account. Or your employer may allow you to automatically deposit portions of your paycheck into multiple accounts. Do it. With twenty-four paychecks per year, just $100 per paycheck will give you an annual $2,400 vacation. That same $100 over just four years will become a $10,000 down payment. $25 per paycheck over 20 years will create a $12,000 fund for a child's wedding. This is, of course, a kind of saving, and is an excellent method of disciplining yourself to achieve financial goals. For goals with a longer timeframe, for example, saving for your child's college education, you can funnel the dollars into a savings or investment account that offers a more substantial ROI, which will enhance whatever contribution you're making.

Saving for Your Kid's Education
When I attended a retreat for women a year or two ago I spoke with Marta, a woman in her late-forties. Marta had a son that was in his second year of college, and she described the financial difficulties she was experiencing in sponsoring her son's education. Marta had put money into an earmarked "529" or college savings account to the tune of $30,000 by the time her son was college age. But this was, apparently, only about a third of the cost of her son's degree program. The son had investigated financial aid and won a small scholarship, but the remaining educational costs were over $50,000. Marta's decision, she confided, had been to pull money out of her home, increasing her personal overhead and restarting the 30-year loan period. In essence she took out a loan to pay for her son's education. This discussion

made me pause. I found myself wondering whether this was or was not a financially sound decision.

Parents often feel obligated to provide for their kids' education, and sometimes for other big-ticket expenses, such as cars, down payments on homes, or big weddings. Certainly, in affluent families doing so is natural and expected. But here again is the question of average, middle-class parents thinking they should be able and trying to do the same things that wealthy people do. Of course, every person has to evaluate and prioritize expenditures related to their children. It may seem, or actually be, a selfless act to sacrifice your own current financial security or to put your future security at risk for the benefit of your child or children's future.

In health or welfare situations, I would not question the decision, but for education, and other large-ticket items like weddings and home purchases, I want to suggest that such "sacrifice" should be carefully examined. As in all financial questions, responsible adults must weigh decisions rationally, particularly if the thing being funded will create or exacerbate debt issues for you or impact your retirement funds. There is no shame in being honest with your budding adult children about the financial constraints around college choices or other big-ticket items and discussing ways to economize.

It's of questionable virtue to portray to your kids a financial capability that you don't really possess. Doing so just perpetuates the inflated lifestyle delusions we discussed in section two. Large-ticket expenditures should only be done to the level of the funds you've allocated for them, and without incurring debt for yourself or jeopardizing your future financial security. I'm not suggesting that parents not help their kids, but I am suggesting that you prepare for likely future events with earmarked savings and to keep your assistance commensurate with those savings and your actual financial status.

As I left that retreat, I reflected on Marta's case, wondering whether her son's eventual career would lead to gracious future support for Marta should she face any financial challenges in retirement. Again, I suppose each person must decide if the possible personal financial challenges are worthwhile. Or might she pay twice? Once now, as she worries about her stretched finances and increased overhead, and again later when she retires and is in reduced circumstances and might require assistance or support?

If you currently have small children whom you later hope to assist in this way, the answer is to responsibly save for those pricey future events. Then calibrate your assistance to the level of the earmarked funds you have allocated.

No Touch Money

Still, as important and responsible as utilizing various types of earmarked savings is, to build wealth you must take your earmarking to the next level. At some point, you need to allocate funds to "no touch" savings. This is where accumulation of wealth begins. Like passively withheld 401(k) money—which is not technically saving but investing, so will be discussed in the next section—directing an amount of money into a savings account that is not to be touched is the starting point of wealth accumulation.

You'll never be wealthy if you can't have money without spending it. Even earmarked savings will be spent for the designated purpose sooner or later. True savings are another animal. The goal of no-touch savings is to build wealth. The beauty of this kind of saving is that, since you do not intend to spend the dollars, at least not until you're using it to help fund a delightful retirement, you're free to place those dollars into longer-term savings vehicles. Longer-term can translate into better ROI. Longer-term also means you can allocate smaller amounts. A $25 per paycheck allocation to a no-touch savings account over just ten years would translate into a $6,000 principal amount, and over 30 years into $18,000. But, and this is a huge but, in those many years with even modest interest added some pretty remarkable things will happen to your savings dollars. So, before we go further let's talk a bit about interest.

Understanding Interest

Banks, credit unions, and online savings institutions generally all offer a variety of interest rates. And when you have a greater time horizon for your savings, you can really shop around to take advantage of the best interest rates available. When considering what to do with your savings, first consider the interest rate and then consider how the rate is compounded.

If the term compound interest means little to you, let's do a quick demonstration of the concept. I've already indicated that a drawback of mattress money is that you will not receive any interest. In some scenarios, you can receive straight, or simple, interest. Here's a quick everyday example: If your cousin asks you for a loan and promises to pay you back with interest in a year, you will get simple interest. You will get back exactly the amount you gave to your cousin, plus exactly "x" percent of that amount as your reward for the loan. Simple interest.

However, most savings institutions compound interest. With compound interest the interest (profit or return) is periodically added to your original investment dollars, and then in the following period you receive interest on the original investment *and on* the added interest. In the next period, you then receive *a bit more interest* due to your larger base amount. Then in the next period you will get a still higher amount of interest because of your slightly larger base amount. And so on. The example (see Figure 4) shows how the same $100 accrues interest over ten years at 10% interest. Now this is an exaggerated example, and you are unlikely to find any savings option today that will offer a 10%

interest rate, but it nicely demonstrates the value in compound interest.

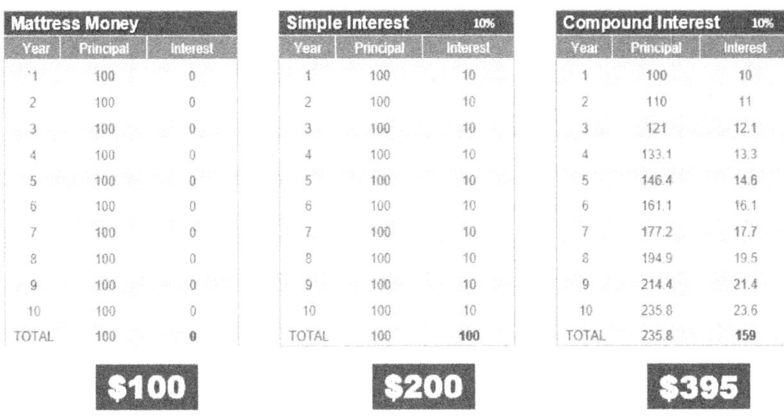

Fig. 4

In the example, the compounding shown is *annual*. That is, the interest is computed and added at the end of each year. In today's world, however, you can find savings accounts that compound interest monthly or even daily. The sooner they add that small amount of interest, the sooner you will be paid interest on the interest. Understanding and taking advantage of compound interest is a foundational lesson in the saving game, particularly understanding that the benefits really begin to accelerate when you can leave your savings alone for long periods, as the example illustrates. That $25 per paycheck I mentioned above having a principal amount grown to $18,000 over thirty years, would actually amount *to about $30,000* if saved with just an average interest rate of 3% over the years with compounding monthly.

So, in placing your dollars in a savings account, you should find out not only the interest rate, but also how often the compounding takes place. The more frequent, the better. Typically, the best interest rates are offered by online savings institutions or on so-called high-yield saving accounts. There may be minimum initial deposits required, and some limit on how frequently you can withdraw funds from the higher-interest accounts, but most people can find such accounts for any savings level.

Certificates of Deposit (CDs)

CDs, or Certificates of Deposit, are generally a promise to leave your money with the institution for a set amount of time, from a few months to a year or more. As a rule, the longer you promise to leave the money alone, the better the interest rate offered. CDs rarely have terms beyond five years. As with any saving, you'll want to evaluate the terms of the CD, considering the interest rate and the compounding frequency.

As a hedge against interest rates rising or falling, "laddering" your CDs is an option to consider: instead of one $10,000 CD, consider placing those funds in five steps of CDs. For example, $2,000 in a one-year CD, $2,000 in a two-year CD, $2,000 in a three-year, and so on. Then if rates go up next year you will have some funds available to reinvest at the higher rate.

Understand there will be early withdrawal penalties if you find you must withdraw the funds from the CD. So, placing funds into CDs can help new savers learn to discipline themselves to leave savings alone. Or, if the lesson has not been learned, to painfully suffer the consequences.

Savings Bonds & Treasury Notes
Savings bonds can be purchased from either state or federal governments through an investment broker. Governments issue bonds to fund specific public works or programs. For some, this is a positive feature that allows you to support your state or federal government initiatives. Bonds were first used during the Great Depression to allow people to support public works programs, and later to support the war effort. U.S. savings bonds are generally considered very safe, being backed by the full faith and credit of the U.S. government. That is, you will get your promised interest, and the principal is safe.

Most bonds, when issued, pay an interest rate comparable to a good CD rate, but no more. Bond interest is typically compounded annually or semi-annually over a given term. Terms are usually long, much longer than CD terms, and are commonly in the fifteen- to thirty-year range. A bond's long term has the benefit of not requiring you to "manage" those dollars of your portfolio at all during that time. So, the bond offers a known return, safety for your dollars, and requires no maintenance. Note that bonds accrue interest only during the term but not after "maturity." When a bond's term date is reached, then, the saver should promptly cash out and move the money into another savings option to continue to accrue interest.

Putting money into bonds guarantees a known interest rate for a very long time. If, over time, the commonly offered interest rates go down, as rates did during and after the Great Recession, your bonds still earn the interest rate you were promised. However, the long term is not such a great benefit if over the years the commonly offered interest rates go up, in which case your dollars will still only make the bond's lower interest rate. Another possible downside of bonds is that they are not usually transferrable unless you die, and they tie up your money for extended periods of time, though they can be redeemed before maturity—with penalties.

If you choose to purchase bonds, make sure to keep good, clear records. Because bonds are such a long-term venture, often bond owners can lose track of them, die before they have matured, and/or not account for them in their financial paperwork or wills. Family members or heirs taking over finances may be unaware or challenged by the need to track down bond terms and redemption processes. In my home, we currently have a stack of old bonds that were inherited from my mother-in-law, but we haven't yet had the wherewithal to figure out the redemption procedures. One estimate puts the value of fully mature but unredeemed bonds in the U.S. at over 1.6 *billion* dollars.

Also consider your personal situation. I started being disciplined in my personal finances later in my life. And I didn't learn about bonds as a savings option until sometime thereafter. Placing money into an investment that would tie up my money for a 15- or 30-year span made little sense to me. You should consider your own work and retirement horizon when determining whether this type of saving is for you.

There are, it should be noted, "bonds" offered by corporations or smaller public institutions, such as cities. While these bonds may be attractive, offering higher interest rates or shorter terms, they will also have greater risk. Companies do fail. Cities can file for bankruptcy. The rule for saving is that your principal should never be at risk. So I essentially discount any bond that is not state or federal. If you do choose to put money into those other types of bonds, you should consider them an investment and recognize there will be risk to your principal—perhaps low risk, but risk, nonetheless.

Treasury notes offered by the U.S. Treasury are similar to bonds. Like government bonds, Treasury notes are considered very safe and offer the added benefit of their interest (the ROI) being exempt from state and local taxes. You usually buy Treasury notes at a discount and redeem them later at full face value, which constitutes the interest.

Treasury notes offer periodic interest, like a bond, and also have the possibility of a discounted purchase price. Terms for Treasury notes rarely exceed 10 years, so Treasury notes are an option that bridges the shorter terms of CDs (up to 5 years) versus government bonds (15 to 30 years).

Why would you consider longer-term saving commitments such as government bonds or Treasury notes? There are good reasons. In Figure 5, you'll see that interest rates for savings (CDs) have fluctuated quite dramatically over the last 35 years.

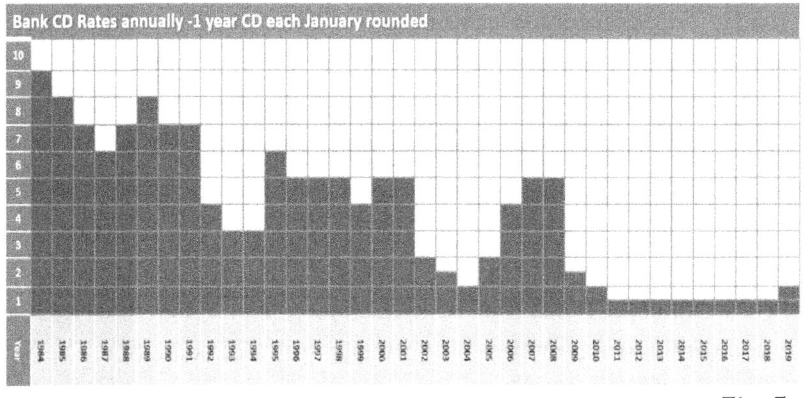

Fig. 5

You can also see in Figure 5 that in recent years return rates have been at historic lows, in most years under 1%. In a moment, we'll consider the impact of inflation on your savings, but for now consider just interest rates and investment terms. If, in 2008, you had locked in a 4% or 5% rate on a 15 or 30-year government savings bond—which was widely available at the time—you would be enjoying an

[154]

ROI significantly better than the going rate today. If you bought your bonds in 2008, at the time of this writing you would have already been receiving that goodly interest rate for over ten years! And, you would have that princely return for many years still to come, so that bond purchase in 2008 would seem like a very smart saving choice! By contrast, if you had placed the money into a 2-year CD, you would have received that 4% or 5% ROI for two years, but thereafter would have made under 2% and often much less. In the last year, rates have crept up slightly but are clearly still hovering near the bottom of the chart, making a long-term commitment to these low-ROI saving options unwise.

Though you never know where the top of the market might be, when rates do rise, as they will, locking in a target ROI with a longer-term commitment can be a part of a good saving strategy, particularly if you're young. What's the magic number that should be locked in? Well, it depends on whether you have other savings dollars available and how you're saving those other dollars. And it depends on whether you can tolerate the possibility of buyer's remorse if rates continue to rise. Once you're locked in, you just have to be at peace with your decision.

Understanding Inflation
I think most people have a general understanding of inflation, but it's important to recognize the relationship between inflation and saving. Inflation, simply put, is any

year-over-year increase in the cost of goods. It refers to the buying power that your dollars have. As a rule, inflation is a one-way street. Over the years, a dollar you earn today will purchase less in the future. For example, when I was a kid, I could take one dollar and purchase two McDonald's hamburgers, fries, and a soda. Today, I can use a dollar to purchase one hamburger at Mickey-D's. The reason I can buy so much less than in my childhood is inflation. Technically, inflation can go both ways. We could have negative inflation, also known as deflation, which we briefly did in 2009 during the Recession. But overall, the usual trend is an edging up of the cost of things and therefore less buying power for your dollar year over year. In some historical cases, inflation was terribly erosive, as in the double-digit inflation our country saw during the 1970s. In most years, however, inflation is a small but progressive chipping away of the value of your dollar (see Figure 6). Still, when inflation rises, we'll generally also see correspondingly higher interest rates for savings, as these economic trends tend to go hand-in-hand.

Inflation Rates					
Year	% inflation	Year	% inflation	Year	% inflation
2019	1.71%	2006	3.24%	1996	2.93%
2018	2.46%	2005	3.39%	1995	2.81%
2017	2.13%	2004	2.68%	1994	2.61%
2016	1.26%	2003	2.27%	1993	2.96%
2015	0.12%	2002	1.59%	1992	3.03%
2014	1.62%	2001	2.83%	1991	4.25%
2013	1.47%	2000	3.38%	1990	5.39%
2012	2.07%	2006	3.24%	1989	4.83%
2011	3.16%	2005	3.39%	1988	4.08%
2010	1.64%	2004	2.68%	1987	3.66%
2009	-0.34%	1999	2.19%	1986	1.91%
2008	3.85%	1998	1.55%	1985	3.55%
2007	2.85%	1997	2.34%	1984	4.30%

Fig. 6

The trick with saving is to try to keep your dollar ROI at or above inflation. In Figure 7, you can see that interest rates paid for savings were generally *higher* than inflation rates for the time frame of the chart through about 2002. But in more recent years the interest rates offered for a saving account, at historic lows, have fallen below the inflation rate. This means that despite your positive ROI from interest, money newly placed in a CD savings account, or the value of that money, even with its added interest, ran at a negative for those years.

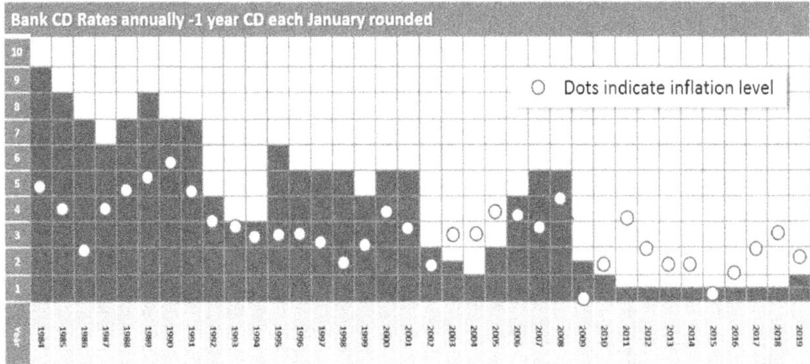

Fig. 7

Don't be too discouraged, though. Saving is a long game, not a short one. Being aware of the history of savings interest, which at one point was almost 10% and has in recent years often hovered well below 1%, you can develop an improved saving strategy. When rates are this low, it's not a time to accept a long-term commitment at the low going rate. So, government bonds and Treasury notes should not be your first choice. Instead, opt for shorter terms, such as those offered on CDs, say one to two years. (Very short terms, such as CDs with terms of a just few months, can be a nuisance, requiring decision-making too frequently.) If rates improve, you'll soon have funds free to take advantage of the uptick in ROI. If rates don't improve, or not significantly, you can renew your CDs in shorter-term savings options. If offered rates reach a number that provides you with a *good* return, you can consider locking in that rate with a longer-term investment like a government bond or Treasury notes.

What is a "good" return rate? In general, any rate that is above the *average* inflation rate of 3% is desirable to preserve, and over time, to grow your principal. I hesitate to direct you to wait to jump into a long-term investment wagon until you can secure a 3% or 4% or 5% rate, though such rates were not uncommon historically. On the other hand, I would never recommend waiting or even hoping for the 10%+ rates we saw during the brief interest lollapalooza in the early 1980s. You have to decide for yourself what rate would tempt you to lock in long term. I'm not anxious to be hammered by readers who: 1) pass by an opportunity to lock in a 2.5% rate; or 2) lock in a seemingly miraculous 4% rate, then find rates continue to rise and now can't take advantage of those even higher rates. Depending on how many dollars you have to place, you might have a strategy of keeping some of your funds available for possible future opportunities and some locked in with a respectable return.

Saving Recap

Saving is your best hedge against the future. Don't let the modest returns from saving fool you. Most financially successful people have a significant percentage of their wealth in savings. There is a reason for this. The money you have in savings is unequivocal wealth. Savings accounts do not fluctuate like investments, which can wildly shrink or grow with the economy or with bad or good luck. Sure, you can and, let's be honest, should allocate some or even most of your dollars to investing to take advantage of the potentially higher yields from the investment options that we will discuss in the next chapter. *But do not bypass or discount this rule.* I've been asked what percent of one's wealth should be allocated to savings versus investments. I can't give an answer other than to say it must be an actual percentage, not a fractional one. Because of the risk involved in investments the savings portion of your wealth is and should be your foundation and security net. Now, let's talk investing.

Rule Four: Invest

My 401K balance went down how much?
-Me, in 2009

Never test the depth of the river with both of your feet.
-Warren Buffet

Investing in Your Future

Let's assume here, then, that you are successfully making money, managing your day-to-day finances well, and setting aside some money in savings. The logical next step is to start investing some of your money. You should remember that investing always involves risk, so I advise some prudence when deciding how to go about investing your available dollars. The prevailing wisdom is that you can invest in riskier vehicles when you're younger, because if there's a dip in the economy or the investment fails, you'll have time to recover financially over subsequent working years. Numerous famous people have shared that they "went bust" at one or more points in their careers. Going bust later in life, however, may be irrecoverable. I think again about that couple I mentioned in last section who ponied up most of their savings to sponsor a later-in-life dream career transition just before the 2020 pandemic, and whose savings and retirement funds were consequently wiped out.

Personal tolerance for risk is also at play. As discussed in the last section, some people are just risk-averse and would stress over any ups and downs in their investment portfolio. They accept lean returns in exchange for the security of knowing that every dollar they set aside will be safe. Even in my own modest investment portfolio, on any given day I may be up or down thousands or even tens of thousands of dollars. At critical dips in the market, I have been "down" amounts in the six figures. If I shared this truth with my spouse, I think some fainting might take place. Such is the nature of investing.

I still find it a bit unsettling when someone enthusiastically shares their investment plans with me when they're not otherwise financially secure. For example, someone with spotty employment who seeks money to invest hoping for big returns, or anyone who places all their savings into an investment scheme. Investing when you are not financially secure is like gambling with your future. It's true that sometimes the risk pays off, but as with any gamble, sometimes you lose your ass. The guidance I provide is based on solid adherence to a financial strategy that will most likely provide you with financial security. Note that the title of this book is not how to miraculously make a million dollars.

Putting All Your Money Anywhere

Before we go into more detail on investing options, I want to reiterate that placing all of your dollars into any investing option, even a government-regulated 401(k), is dangerous. You should always allocate some funds to safe savings. It's fine to use a 401(k) as your only mode of investing, as we'll indicate below. But even funds placed in a ubiquitous 401(k) can suffer a serious downturn in value.

As already mentioned, during the last two significant economic downturns, the 2000 Dot-Com Bust and the Great Recession of 2007-2010, I saw 25% and 40% respectively of my invested dollars evaporate. In subsequent years, my portfolio did, of course, rebound and eventually surpassed the pre-downturn high mark, but those troubled years were very hard on my emotions. Luckily, I still had sufficient working years ahead of me to recover. Now, being significantly closer to retirement age, I've *already* shifted a much larger percentage of my portfolio toward less risk and beefed-up traditional savings accounts.

Losing 40% or more of your retirement dollars when it's almost time to start tapping the funds can dramatically alter your entire retirement plan. In the investment world, and particularly in the stock market, such dips *will* occur periodically and inevitably. A wise man said, and I paraphrase, *"Never check the depth of investing waters with both feet."*

Investing Options
401(k) Plans

For investing options, let's start with the must-do investing. If you have a 401(k) plan available through your employer, sign up. Allocate as much as you possibly can to the plan. Be sure to enroll for at least the "matched" percentage offered by your company. This is usually 3 to 6 percent. Failing to sign up for that matched amount is like leaving cash on the table. Be aware that it often takes a few years to "vest" in the matched dollars, meaning that the matched dollars aren't yours until you stay with the company for a few years. But after those years, this is a 3 to 6% extra cash-money gift to you annually. Don't leave it on the table! The dollars *you* contribute are, of course, always yours.

The money you allocate to a 401(k) is pre-tax, and you benefit from this in two ways. First, your taxable income will be seen as lower because some of your income was shifted, before being taxed, to the retirement account. So your annual tax bill will be lower. And second, you reap returns on 100% of the dollars you put in. When you take money from your paycheck to save or invest somewhere, you're using after-tax dollars, which are, in fact, actually reduced about 20% because you paid that much in taxes to get those dollars. The 401(k) dollars are invested before any taxes are paid, so you're investing about 20% more and getting returns on that invested amount right from the start.

Of course, taxes on income are inevitable, but you won't owe tax on the 401(k) dollars until you withdraw them, presumably in retirement. When you withdraw any dollars from the retirement account, at that point, those dollars will count as taxable income in the withdrawal year. The hope is that you'll be retired and will only withdraw a bit at a time. If so, you'll only owe taxes on your modest withdrawals as a retired person, so this also works to your benefit tax-wise. If you withdraw the money before retirement, you'll owe income taxes on it, of course, and you may also owe a penalty for "early withdrawal" if you're under age 59½. 401(k)s are federally protected *retirement* savings plans, so you'll be penalized if withdrawing money for purposes other than retirement.

I strongly suggest you never withdraw money from a 401(k) before retirement. With 30 to 40 years of career, you're likely to vest in at least one and in all likelihood a few plans. Personally, I have five company 401(k) plans. 401(k) funds can generally remain in an employer's plan if the dollars in the account are over a threshold amount—typically $5,000. In my career moves, I kept my money in the various 401(k) institutions rather than "rolling over" the dollars. My thinking was that I was getting some beneficial diversification in my investment portfolio by keeping my dollars in the assorted plans, which offer different investment options. Unless your company uses an off-brand provider, your 401(k) money is safe.

If your 401(k) balance when you leave an employer is less than $5,000, and you're sent a distribution check, don't just take the check and spend it. Nor can you just deposit the check in a traditional savings account. As mentioned, if you spend it or fail to keep it in a retirement account, you'll owe income taxes on the money, and possibly penalties. Instead, deposit that check into your new employer's 401(k) or open an IRA, which we'll discuss in a moment. You've already gone through the pain of setting those dollars aside. Don't waste that effort, which might represent years of financial willpower. Furthermore, cashing out a 401(k)—or any no-touch account—is not just about losing the face value of that account and possibly paying penalties. The more important issue is that you lose all the future returns that, as demonstrated in the last section, make saving and investments so potentially lucrative.

In the last section we talked about "no touch" dollars. 401(k) money should be in that category. To illustrate, for one of my shorter employment stints, my 401(k) was just over $5,000 when I left the job. If I had cashed out at that point, I would have taken home less than $4,000 after taxes and penalties. Instead, I left the money in that company's 401(k) plan. Today that same account is worth over $21,000. I had already gone through the pain of withholding and saving that money. Cashing it out for no good reason means I would have missed out on returns of over $15,000(!) and more dollars still to come. Another example: my earliest 401(k) was under $20,000 when I left, and reflected *six years* of modest savings, plus the company's matching funds contributions. That account suffered greatly during both of the recessions I've weathered, and for a time was worth substantially *less* than when I left the former employer. But today it is nevertheless worth about $76,000. This is not bragging about my money; this is a real-life example that demonstrates that if you don't touch your 401(k) money, good things can happen.

401(k) Investment Options

Nowadays most 401(k) plans offer simplified investment choices that align with an employee's retirement timeline, for example, a Retirement 2030 fund or a Retirement 2040 fund, etc. Such funds are managed risk-wise based on the employee's time horizon and projected retirement date, choosing investments with less risk when retirement is closer. You are not tied to any fund in a 401(k), however, and if you want to be more or less aggressive you can select a target retirement fund further in the future with more risk, or one closer to the target date with less risk. If you don't select one of these retirement-target funds, or if such funds are not offered by your provider, you will have to choose your own investments from the selection offered for your company.

Sadly, this is often where I lose people. Having to select the funds for your 401(k) portfolio is almost stressful enough to put some people off the entire process. Figure 8 offers a few guidelines:

Large cap funds / blue chip funds	Funds of assorted stock comprised of a mix of big, well-established businesses.	Usually, performance is aligned with the Dow Jones Industrial Average. If the Dow's up, so would these funds be. If the Dow's down, these funds would also be down.
Small cap	Funds of assorted smaller companies' stock.	Performance may reflect more variation based on the talent or luck behind the fund manager's choices.
Foreign investment	No surprise: funds of assorted foreign companies' stock.	Also, may reflect more variation based on the talent or luck behind the fund manager's choices, and usually aligned with performance of associated international markets.
Commodities	Funds investing in precious metals, like gold and silver, energy resources, such as oil and natural gas, and agricultural goods, such as wheat. (Note: not every 401(k) offers a commodity fund.)	Performance is aligned with global prices and on the on the talent or luck behind the fund manager's choices.
Bonds	A fund comprised of mixed bonds: some safe-as-houses government bonds, purchased and maturing at various times, plus assorted other bonds with more variable returns.	Less risk to your dollars but usually also lower return over the long term. Generally better returns than individual bonds, as discussed in the savings section, due to the bond maturity variety and mix of bond types.
Money market	Not usually a true money market account but a fund that invests in a mix of money market accounts. Look for a fund that has MM or "money market" in its name.	By far the safest place in your 401(k). Rare for MM funds to ever go negative. But *very* low returns comparatively over the long haul.
Company stock	Most public companies allow 401(k) investment in your company stock as an option, though laws now limit the percentage of the allocation. This is to protect employees from going bust if the company goes bust.	Obviously, returns are correlated with the company's performance.

Fig 8

People have asked me how they should allocate the money in their 401(k). I really cannot answer that question specifically. You must consider your current financial situation, other savings or investments. and your goals. Plus, of course, your risk tolerance and time horizon.

People also ask if they should consult a financial advisor. I personally have had mixed results talking to "professionals" about my investments. Most advisors have goals and incentives through their organizations that impede their ability to simply provide helpful advice. Here is an example. I called a large investment company where one of my 401(k)s is held. Because I am now over 59½, I can access my 401(k) dollars without penalties, and I wanted to move some of my dollars out of "investment" and into "savings." My desire was based on my tiered plan to shift chunks of my invested dollars into lower-risk options, and to pay taxes on chunks of retirement dollars in advance of retirement. I spent about 30 minutes on the phone with a financial advisor whose credentials were impressive—he told me all about them—but who tried to convince me that a Roth IRA at his institution was a better option than transferring my funds to a savings account. I spent a good number of years working in sales, and I know a "close" when I hear one. This guy tried to close me on the IRA. Then, when I would not agree, he spent time trying to close me on a free in-person appointment with one of their local financial planners. I do not think this guy was trying to do me any harm financially, and the Roth IRA was not a bad idea. But the bigger point is that this institutional financial advisor had an agenda, and the agenda was clearly to stop me from withdrawing any of my funds to reinvest elsewhere.

Another friend who retired recently shared that she spoke with an internal advisor to set up monthly distributions from her 401(k) funds and was given a rather hard-sell pitch to purchase an annuity. Of course, you must speak to an advisor when you need to make such arrangements, but, when doing so always weigh their advice carefully, with awareness that they might not have only your best interests in mind. Also, don't allow yourself to be "closed" on an option or course that you didn't plan for or request. Always ask for time to consider their proposals. Then conduct your own research or seek independent counsel regarding their suggestions. In my case, I found that a Roth IRA *was* a viable option for me, but the annuity suggestion for my friend would have essentially consumed all her savings, limited her financial options in retirement and only offered a modest income.

For people who desire financial planning assistance and direction, the prevailing wisdom is to speak to a certified, independent, fee-based financial planner, not an advisor affiliated with an institution, no matter how impressive their credentials. In truth, even some independent financial advisers might have associations or biases that could skew the impartiality of their advice. But you can find reputable financial planners. Always check references and reviews for anyone you choose to trust for financial advice.

For your 401(k) allocations, some providers offer a "managed" account option. This means that the institution will collect a small fee from your account and periodically review how your investments are doing. The review will take your age and retirement horizon into account. This sounds good, right? But those management fees do eat away at your returns, and you will pay the fees even if no adjustments are needed. Furthermore, the "managing" sometimes translates into shifts in your portfolio, and shifts sometimes involve fees, so there goes a little more of your returns. People generally sign on for a managed account because they feel unprepared to make their own decisions about the investment options, which is fine. You do not need to worry that their adjustments will ever really harm you. In fact, a managed account is only adjusted or rebalanced based on conventionally established algorithms and guidelines, but there will be a cost involved with such services.

My advice for average people is either to simply select a retirement target fund, if offered, or if not, just select a random mix from your options. Make it a mix of some percentage of one or more stock funds—more risk, but higher return potential—and some percentage of bond funds—lower risk, but consistently lower returns. Your 401(k) institution will typically display the performance of each fund over the past year, over the past 5 years, and since inception. Beware of selecting just one fund that has performed well historically, or, even riskier, one that performed well just recently. Investment should be done with a long-term vision, so don't be swayed only by recent performance. Start with your best-guess selection mix and see how you do. Most institutions display a chart of your allocations and their categories and indicate if your choices are more or less risky than is recommended for your age. You can adjust if you want better risk alignment. This is part of becoming more financially savvy. Be aware that excessive shifting of your funds around in your 401(k) can incur fees, as just mentioned above, and fees impact your portfolio's performance. So, resist the urge to over-manage a 401(k). Annual or semi-annual reviews should suffice. If you see that your returns are good, stay the course. If you see that your investments are not performing as well as, say, the Dow, then make small shifts in your allocations.

As suggested earlier, a 401(k) may be, for some, the only stock market investment they ever have. *There is nothing wrong with that.* 401(k) investing utilizes a solid investment vehicle easily managed by most people. Your 401(k) funds are also well regulated and federally insured, keeping your dollars safe from any organizational disruption or failures. A company pension can go bust, but your dollars in a company's 401(k) plan are legally protected from any impingement. For average folks, I strongly recommend utilizing any 401(k) plan available to you to the fullest capability. As of this writing, you can personally contribute up to $19,500 annually and an additional $6,500 in catch-up contributions if you're over 50. There's really no reason to seek other investment opportunities if you're not fully participating in a 401(k).

If you can, consider an automatic annual increase in your 401(k) allocation. This option is offered by many institutions. The idea is to allot at least some of any annual wage increase you receive into increasing your 401(k) dollars. The goal, of course, is to increase the amount you are funneling into the 401(k) until you are contributing the maximum allowed.

Still, not everyone works for a company that offers this benefit. The self-employed, independent contractors, and those working for small companies may not be offered a handy company-sponsored 401(k) retirement plan. What then?

IRAs/Roth IRAs

In the absence of a company-sponsored 401(k), individuals do have retirement fund investing available through IRAs (individual retirement accounts) or Roth IRAs, discussed below. Unfortunately, individuals are significantly limited in the dollars amounts they may contribute to these tax deferred accounts. As of this writing, you can contribute just $6,500 annually or $7,500 if you are over 50. Like 401(k) money, the dollars you put into an IRA are pre-tax. That is, the dollars are subtracted from your taxable income to lower your taxes now, but when you withdraw the dollars later, in retirement, you will have to pay taxes on them as income. As with a 401(k), you'll have assorted investment options. Often the IRA will have more choices than a company 401(k), which might seem like a benefit, but can be a bit confusing to those who want simplicity. The categories and choices are similar to 401(k)s, so you can use the instructions from that section to guide you with IRA investing.

Roth IRAs allow you to contribute after-tax dollars into an account where the money is allowed to grow without tax consequences. The important benefit of a Roth IRA is that because you use dollars that have already been taxed, you can later withdraw the dollars without owing taxes. The contribution limits for Roth IRAs are the same as for the traditional IRA, and you can't double dip. You can contribute up to the maximum only in an IRA or a Roth IRA, though you can do a mix between traditional and Roth IRAs as you prefer. Furthermore, generally you can only contribute to an IRA if you are not participating in a 401(k). I should mention that there are some sophisticated "back door" options for funneling or converting dollars into Roth IRAs but that is an advanced finance process, so if interested seek professional advice.

Self-Employed Retirement Saving Options

If you are self-employed or own a small business and want to be more aggressive in saving for retirement there are some significantly more expansive options available than IRAs. If self-employed, consider a SEP-IRA which can allow you to save up to 25% of your income, capped at $58,000, annually. SIMPLE IRA are an option for small businesses which provide for employee contributions up to $13,500 plus $3,000 catch-up for those over 50 years old and requiring a mandatory employer matching contribution. Note that since SIMPLEs require a matching percentage and for the business to offer the benefit to all employees, cost to the business must be considered. There are also so-called Solo 401(s) with high contribution potential, up to $58,000, but more complex set-up and administration requirements.

Buying a House

I have been asked whether buying a house is better than putting money into a retirement account. My typical answer is that most financially responsible adults need to do both. While all the discussion about handling your housing costs in the section on managing your finances are valid, there are good financial reasons to purchase a home. Assuming you are already solidly adhering to the three preceding rules: you are consistently working, managing your day-to-day expenses, and saving some dollars, a home purchase is usually a good idea.

The reason purchasing makes so much sense if you are solid in your finances is that most people will have housing costs anyway. Rent is a straight expense, but a purchased home is a potential investment. If you can swing the cost to get into a home purchase, then your monthly housing expense offers some quite substantial perks.

First, you can potentially deduct some or all of the interest from your mortgage on your taxes. In recent years, tax structures have changed, so that the "standard" deduction for average income people has been raised. If your mortgage is modest, you may not necessarily be eligible to itemize your deductions and use the interest deduction against your taxes. In markets where home prices are higher, however, you'll likely be paying more in interest than the standard deduction and can partake of a deduction for mortgage interest, reducing your tax bill every year.

There's also the advantage of having a known and invariable housing cost and location. Rents can go up, sometimes dramatically, or an owner could choose not to continue to offer you the rental. You might then have to pay significantly higher rent for the same location or amenities. Or, conversely, you might have to accept fewer amenities or a less preferable location to maintain a similar overhead. With a mortgage, your housing cost and location are known quantities with only slight variability.

Of course, the most significant perk of purchasing a home is that your payment every month actually moves you toward genuine ownership of the property. A typical mortgage is 30 years, so if you just pay the mortgage every month, you can potentially own the house, free and clear, after 30 years. If you purchase at, say, age 35, you can have a home for retirement with no monthly payment by age 65. Nice, right? Add a little extra to your monthly payment every month, and you can pay off the mortgage in significantly fewer years. There are some handy calculators online that can show you how a small extra amount added each month will impact your loan term. To find a calculator just Google "mortgage pay-down calculator."

A final possible perk of a home purchase is that your home is likely to go up in value. I say likely, but like any investment, appreciation is not guaranteed. Home prices, like the stock market, go up and down. The goal would be to purchase when home prices are in a lull and reap the rewards of your home gaining in value. When people express too much concern about whether they are buying at a good time, I usually remind them that the most important factor is not what pricing is happening in the housing market. The most important factor is that they have a solid financial foundation for a home purchase and are purchasing as part of a long-term financial strategy, not as a real estate speculator.

In general, a primary residence is a sensible purchase for most people, particularly over the long haul. Look for a home that makes financial sense for your budget and where you will be happy. Over time, if the home is satisfying to you, your monthly payment will lead to the great benefit of actual ownership. If over time the home also appreciates in value, look at that as the cherry on top of the ice-cream sundae.

Second Homes

Second homes are another matter. While you may still be eligible for an interest deduction on a second home, often their resale value or prospects for appreciation are less assured, particularly if the second home is truly some little cabin in the woods or similar vacation property. If you need to get your money out of the second home, know that selling seasonal or vacation homes is sometimes more difficult. In tough times, when you might most need to liquidate, other people will also be tightening their belts, and there will be fewer buyers looking for an indulgence property. Also be aware that any renting out of that property beyond about 14 days a year will potentially "convert" the second home into a rental or mixed-use status and force you to into very different type of financial accounting. Later in this chapter, we'll discuss real estate and rental properties as an investment.

Time-Shares

Time-shares, so popular in the 1980s and 90s, are another animal altogether. Time-shares are only occasionally a true second home, meaning rarely do you actually own a percentage of any real property. More often you just purchase an "interest in" a real estate consortium. This is why many time-shares allow you to choose from a variety of locations for your vacation time. Resale value of a time-share is usually meager, not uncommonly at a loss overall. If you consider a time-share at all, just treat it as a vacation purchase, certainly not an investment, no matter what the salesman tells you.

Individual Stocks

Another common question is whether to play the stock market. I always tell friends and family that they should "invest" fully through their 401(k) or an IRA before considering other investing. Still, having a stock portfolio is a common investment option, and certainly fortunes have been made (and lost) in the stock market. So, let's talk about investing in individual stocks.

Once upon a time company-sponsored 401(k)s allowed employees to invest all of their 401(k) retirement dollars in the company's stock. This was intended to demonstrate confidence in the success of the company, and employees were encouraged to allocate at least some or all of their retirement dollars to the company's stock. In more recent years, new laws have severely restricted this practice. The reason for the restriction is to protect employees from over-committing their retirement funds to a single company's performance. Allow me to illustrate.

I have generally chosen to not mention companies I worked for, but in this case, I will make an exception. During the 1990s, I worked for Fannie Mae. During that time Fannie Mae offered a unique employee benefit of a stock option purchase plan. While offering stock options to executives is not uncommon, back then, all Fannie Mae employees were awarded a modest annual allocation of stock options. Fannie Mae stock at that time was doing quite well, and I knew many employees who annually scraped together the cash to purchase the stocks. I, myself, purchased some of the discounted stocks. In those boon years, many average employees amassed impressive portfolios of Fannie Mae stock, and those portfolios, in some cases, were the primary basis of the employee's retirement portfolio. One manager I worked for bragged that she had a *million dollars*' worth of Fannie Mae stock in the late 1990s, because she had purchased the stock consistently over her many years with the company.

You may know where this story is going. During the dot-com recession of the early 2000s, Fannie Mae stock took a moderate hit, from a high of over $70 per share to under $50. Though I no longer worked for Fannie Mae at that time, I thought about my co-worker and how her million dollars' worth of stock was likely being reduced. However, soon thereafter Fannie Mae stock rebounded and enjoyed new highs during the early to mid-2000s, at one point reaching $85 per share.

Then the Great Recession hit. Quite suddenly, in 2008, Fannie Mae stock tanked. Based on bad press over sub-prime mortgage practices and talk of a government take-over, Fannie Mae stock prices declined to under $1 per share. I do not know if that former co-worker was able to anticipate the Great Recession and its impact on the mortgage world, or whether she was able to sell off all or most of her stock before it became almost worthless. But *that's* the stock market, and that's why 401(k)s no longer allow employees to invest heavily in their company's stock. It involves too much risk to have all your eggs in one basket, as they say. Even big, popular, or long-standing companies like Fannie Mae can plunge in value. In some cases, the company can recoup to pre-downturn levels, as Fannie Mae did during the early 2000s, but you can never know with certainty when a catastrophic downturn is coming. Even as I write this, many years later, Fannie Mae is trading at under $4 per share. You absolutely cannot be guaranteed any single stock's future worth.

Obviously, putting together a portfolio of individual company stocks will have less risk than just owning one company's stock, but stock markets are cyclical and the market, as a whole, can periodically take dramatic hits. I'm doing some edits to this chapter after a week when the Dow Jones Industrial Average lost over 12% of its value, and I'm a bit nervous, as you might expect, to see what next week will bring. I assure you my little stock portfolio was hit pretty hard, as were most other people's. That's the nature of investing in stocks.

In the wealth-building game, any year you are not going forward, you are going backward. For future security, you want your investments to consistently grow, so that you're receiving a return on your investment, that is, growth of your invested amount. Losing money, or eroding of the principal amount, as happens with stocks in some years, will cost you more than just the loss of the principal. It costs you all the years of additional returns you would have made on the growth dollars as well. Go back to the savings chart and look at it again. The secret and often underappreciated benefit of savings versus investing is in the steady forward momentum of savings.

And while the overall stock market always, eventually, recovers, specific stocks may not. Earlier in this book, I mentioned that I currently hold a small portfolio of individual stocks. Occasionally, I buy stock based on some idiosyncratic bit of news. Sometimes it's paid off, and sometimes it hasn't. About ten years ago I bought a small amount of stock called BioAmber based on an article that mentioned biotech as an up-and-coming industry. The stock never did perform particularly well. After a first promising year of slight improvement, in subsequent years the price actually eroded to about half of the price I paid for the stock. As a vigilant investor, I monitor the stocks in my portfolio in an app on my phone. Over time I did notice some further deterioration of the BioAmber stock price. Still, I didn't have a great deal of money invested, was not too concerned, and continued to hope for a recovery. Then BioAmber just dropped off my app's reporting. I checked the stock news. Yep, it was gone. Filed bankruptcy—closed its doors. Total loss.

So, am I telling you not to invest in the stock market? No. There's a good chance that over time you will make money with a diverse stock portfolio. And over the long term the stock market certainly offers the potential for significantly higher returns than savings. However, when a stock market downturn occurs, *as it will*, you do not want all of your accumulated wealth at risk. People killed themselves after the stock market crash of 1929, literally jumped off bridges or buildings. I recommend that you allocate a prudent percentage of your wealth to remaining just that: wealth. Safely secured in savings institutions or instruments. Then, of course, manage your investments and adjust your strategy as your life circumstances change.

Day Trading

The proliferation of low-cost online trading capabilities has led to an explosion of day trading of individual stocks. Day trading is purchasing stocks to hold for very short terms, then selling to make quick profits. The only way to make large sums in this manner is to "invest" large sums. Day traders often make their trades on margin, that is, only putting up a fraction of the trade cost to cover the bet, and having the rest covered on what is essentially credit. Then, if the price of the selected stock or stocks perform as hoped, the day's profit is assured. As you might expect, however, sometimes the hoped-for rise (or fall) in value does not occur, and day traders can be caught frantically juggling trades and debts when the market doesn't go their way. Day trading is clearly risky business and can lead to problems akin to gambling addiction. As an investment option, I would say, use only dollars specifically allocated to the activity, and make sure that your other wealth vehicles are secure.

Gold, Other Precious Metals & Bitcoin

I've lumped these options together because they all involve alternate currencies that fluctuate in value. The investing strategy here, as with individual stocks, is for the gold, platinum or other precious metal, or Bitcoin to appreciate or improve in price and grow the value of the invested dollars. First let's use gold as the example. Remember, any investment involves risk. Figure 9 shows how gold has traded over the past 35 years. Clearly, gold has experienced a few remarkable runs, for example, the stretch between 2009 and 2012 at the tail end of the Great Recession, when gold rose quickly over three years from about $800 per ounce to a high of over $1,800 per ounce. Lucky were those investors who already held significant amounts in gold during that particular boon time. As I write this, gold is trading for about $1,200, somewhat diminished but still quite high. Are we likely to see a skyrocket in gold prices again? Who knows, but clearly you cannot have absolute confidence that an investment in gold or other variable currency will translate into a guaranteed return. Owning gold or other precious metals, it should be noted, involves actually *possessing* the gold or metal—versus a commodities fund in precious metals in your 401(k). The coins, gold bars, or jewelry must be kept secure, as possession is the only assurance of ownership and value. As mentioned in the saving section, theft is a real concern with any currency that is kept in your home, so with gold or any other precious metal, security must be taken into account.

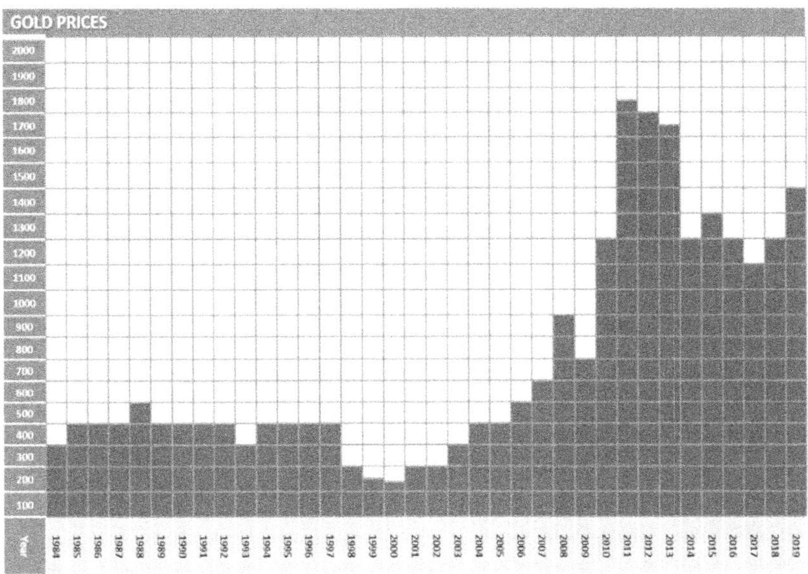

Fig. 9

Bitcoin, on the other hand, is crypto-currency. It has no physical existence or national affiliation. Bitcoin's basis is an amount of the currency itself, electronically documented upon purchase. Gold hoarders may scoff at this electronic currency, anticipating a time when the only true currency will be a currency you can handle and trade. But today *most* currencies are just pieces of paper or nominal coins that represent some allocated value. That the US dollar is backed by actual gold is only fractionally true today.

The value of the currency you own is an amount computed based on the current traded value for each full Bitcoin share, just like any other currency, such as the dollar or euro. Bitcoin has had quite a ride in recent years, compared to its early years when Bitcoin remained at or near par value. Figure 10 shows Bitcoin's astounding appreciation in the past few years. Bitcoin remains an interesting investment case study, and its future, and that of other independent currencies remains to be seen. Maybe the currency of the future or maybe a passing fad.

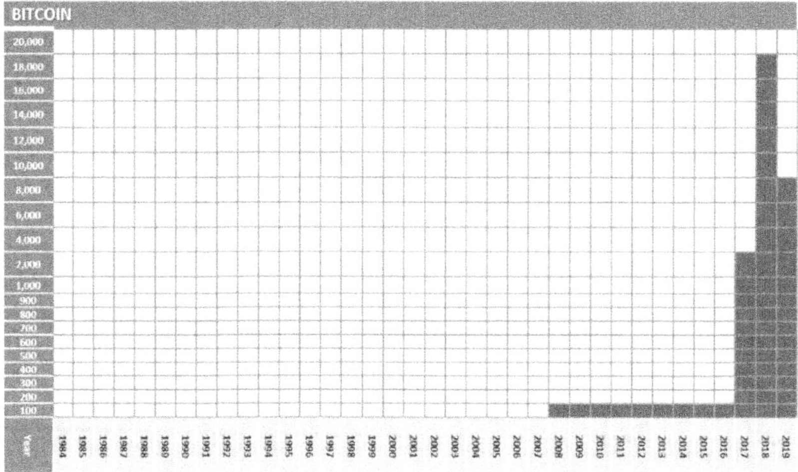

Fig. 10

As with any investment, you hope to purchase currency at a time when the value is lower and ride a wave of appreciation. But there is no a guarantee. If this is an investment option you want to pursue, I suggest balancing it, as always, with safer saving options and possibly other investment options as well. As with individual stocks, it is always extremely risky to allocate too much of your wealth to a single investment.

Real Estate Investing

Two types of real estate investing are worth discussing. One is house-flipping and the other is purchasing investment property for rental income.

Flipping Houses

Though popularized these days by cable television shows, flipping houses has been around for many years. In the 1990s I worked in REO (Real Estate Owned) and became acquainted with a number of investors who bought, fixed up, and sold foreclosure homes. Can this be lucrative? Sure. Is it risky? Yes, it is. I worry about people who decide to "invest" money in flipping when they are not otherwise secure financially or when they have little or no particular real estate knowledge or construction experience. To successfully flip, you need to have money to initially purchase the fixer-upper, to cover the cost of the trade labor and materials for improvements, and to meet the holding cost of the property until you re-sell. You also must have a cadre of trusted sub-contractors or a competent, dedicated general contractor to manage the rehab. The margin of profit, the difference between all the costs totaled and final sale price, is often narrow. Unforeseen expenses or a slow-down in the market can wipe out the profits or possibly leave you with a loss. New or hopeful flippers rarely wish to consider this truth, but if you chat with a career flipper, they'll always have stories about nightmare houses with significant losses.

If this type of "investing" is of interest to you, I suggest you become licensed in real estate, at minimum. Usually, licensing requires little more than a class or two and an exam. Further, you should not consider a paid one-day seminar on flipping houses as genuine training. There's a reason those people are conducting seminars. If they were successfully flipping, they wouldn't need to collect money from yokels at a seminar who want to learn how to get rich quick by flipping houses. They are making money on you, not the other way around.

Despite my cautions, some people will attempt to flip houses. Be prepared for a learning curve, and don't risk any more than you can afford to lose. In short-term real estate speculation, which is what flipping is, you most certainly can lose some or all of your invested dollars. Make sure all the other rules of finance are solid before shelling out money to "invest" in this fashion. If you're trying to do this as a career move, as with any other self-employment, you should have a solid Plan B in place.

Investment Property Ownership

Purchasing real estate as investment property is quite different from flipping. The intention with investment property is to hold the property and, ostensibly, to have an income from it. The type of property you purchase can vary. You might purchase single family houses, condominiums, vacation properties, smaller multi-family properties (two to four units), or even apartment buildings. Or you could invest in commercial real estate or land. You don't necessarily need to be an active landlord either because property management companies are abundant, though unsurprisingly will take a cut of the income.

Success in real estate investing is contingent upon doing a thorough assessment of the investment. In real estate investing, there are several standard methods to define the acceptable cost basis to income valuation based on multipliers or other calculations. How to successfully purchase income property for investing is covered in depth in other books and is beyond the scope of this section.

I would, however, like to offer two observations on investment property. One, as with most investing, investment property is rarely a get-rich-quick with no effort scenario. Make sure you are comfortable with the number of dollars you allocate and with the risk. I had a friend in California who participated in a "program" to purchase rental properties in a depressed Midwestern state for very little money. This was presented with the promise of endless rental income returns, managed at no cost or effort to the investor. For a time, she assured me that the rental money was indeed coming in every month, albeit in low amounts. She stopped talking about it after about a year. I suspect that either the "investment" stopped producing, went bust, or she pulled out. I don't know if she actually lost money, but I feel pretty confident that she didn't make much.

Two, if you are investing with a true, comfortable long-term plan, you'll probably be alright. Like the stock market, over the long term, real estate generally offers a profit. But remember that dollars tied up in real estate are not easily accessed in a crunch. Cashing out too soon or while in crisis can wipe out the hoped-for returns on your invested dollars. In any calculations for investment property, it usually takes *years* before you realize a return or profit, since you first have to recoup your invested dollars.

When considering any investing, particularly when investing significant dollars, your decision should always compare the potential for returns for this particular investment against how those same dollars would perform for you in an entirely safe savings vehicle. Then compare more mainstream, safer investing options, like 401(k)s or IRAs. If you are already well funded in savings and retirement accounts, then perhaps you do have money to gamble on real estate. And, as I mentioned above, assuming your initial calculations are good, you will probably do just fine in the long term.

Art or Collectibles
When considering possible investment opportunities for your money, maybe you are drawn to the world of original art or collectibles. As we see in the media, wealthy people do sometimes purchase art pieces or some type of collectible and consider them investments. Average folks,

however, need to be realistic about placing money into art or collectibles. Most often, even the wealthy gravitate toward such "investing" because they enjoy the art or items they collect. Rarely is such investing a strategy for actually realizing profits.

Don't fool yourself about putting money into art or collectibles as an investment. Be honest. If you just want to buy something you admire or receive pleasure from owning, admit that and decide if you can afford to purchase the item. But do not try to convince yourself (or your spouse) that such purchases are investments. In some cases, art or collectibles *can* be sold if you need money. Occasionally the sale of a particular piece of art or of a selected collectible can even make you a profit. Far more commonly, though, are situations where you are unable to convince others to pay what you are sure the item is worth, even if you have had it appraised. The most common outcomes when you try to cash out on art or collectibles are *modest* gains and occasional losses. For most people, purchasing art or collectibles isn't really an investment. In most cases, it's just a purchase, with some possible resale value.

I have one friend whose husband collected old tools, toys, and early electronic gadgets. He purchased "lots" from estates or dealers "as an investment." He insisted that he would reap significant profits selling off the individual items. To be fair, he did work a booth at a monthly swap meet, where he tried to make a profit on these "collectibles." Yet, he had filled their garage and later a rented storage unit with these supposedly valuable investment items. The sales at the swap meet generally covered his fees and usually the monthly rental on the storage. But remember, as in all things financial, you must assess the entire picture. What was this guy's time worth, all those hours sitting in a booth at the swap meet? Even if he walked away after a long day with a few hundred dollars, which would have been a big day, he still had to deduct the swap meet fees, storage rental, initial purchase cost, and his time. In the final analysis, this was a hobby. He just liked old gadgets, toys, and tools.

To follow through on this story, let me say here that it is okay to want to buy the art, those collectibles, or even "lots" of gadgets, but do so honestly and with awareness of your overall financial capabilities. If you are neglecting to put sufficient or any money toward savings or retirement, then such spending may be frivolous and can't be dressed up in the garb of an investment.

Other People's Business

If you are a person who appears to be successful, you may at some point be approached to invest in another person's business. Seed money, silent partnering, or so-called angel investing is a real thing. Many people watch the hit television show *Shark Tank* with interest. When I was trying to drum up attention for my "Open Airways Acupressure Pillow," I attended a couple angel-investor events for inventors. Investment requests like this happen surprisingly often in circles of friends and families. I had a close friend who asked several of her well-heeled friends to invest so she could open her own hair salon. My own brother accepted seed money for many years from a long-standing silent partner to purchase pumpkins and trees for his annual pumpkin-patch and Christmas-tree-lots business. And in both of these cases the businesses were successful, and the investment returns delivered.

Investing in other people's business is not always successful, however. You might earn a promised return or profit. Or, the business might not be successful, and your returns might never materialize. You could possibly even lose the principal amount invested. Whatever you decide, make sure to treat it as a business arrangement. Get the terms in writing. Ask yourself how you will handle things if they don't turn out as promised.

When you put money into someone else's business as an investment, you're usually risking more than just the money. If the venture goes awry, people sometimes end up in court or develop deep antipathy over such financial entanglements. Investing in other people's business is a game best played by those with plenty of money in the bank, who can literally afford to lose the money if the worst happens. They may still feel frustration or anger if the investment doesn't pan out, but they won't be ruined by it. I enjoy watching true crime shows, and I wonder about victims that allowed their finances to be bankrupted by some "business partner," or people whose financial lives were destroyed when they shelled out all their savings for some ultimately disreputable business venture. Good financial management means you never invest unless you are otherwise secure financially.

The Bank of You

Closely related to investing in the businesses of others is simply loaning money. Again, if you seem to be financially stable, requests of this nature may come to you. In the managing and saving chapters, we discussed spending money on your children's big-ticket items: college, weddings, etc. In those cases, you were simply making decisions about spending your dollars, in essence giving this money to your children.

But what of requests that are presented as a request for a "loan"? I have been approached several times by friends or family members with such a request. This is awkward, and the risk I mentioned above about potential antipathy is quite real if the loan is not repaid or repaid in a timely manner or with promised interest. I had one friend balk at paying back some money, who actually asked, "Do you need it?" As if I was only entitled to repayment of the money if I was in financial distress. I never did receive the money, and we're no longer friends. I also had the experience of a family member who diligently paid me back on a loan, as promised.

I caution parents about spending money on children if they're putting their day-to-day finances or retirement plans in jeopardy. Lending money requires even more caution. Lending money, even if interest is offered, is not a reliable way to make money for yourself. It most certainly isn't "investing." It's a favor to others. When someone asks to borrow money, it's because they don't have whatever money is needed. This makes giving them a loan quite risky. I know of numerous cases where some family member in grim financial circumstances "borrowed" money from a more stable family member or friend. For rent, for school, for a car, for a business, for an attorney, for bail. Seldom have I seen this turn out well. The pain and awkwardness of declining to give the loan is sharp but quick. It's true that the refusal could end the relationship. However, the pain of a lingering, unpaid debt lasts much longer, and may likewise sour the relationship.

Lending money is not investing. Do it for love, if you are willing and able, but understand that you are risking not only your dollars but the relationship as well.

Investing Conclusion

In this book, investing is presented as the fourth of the four rules of personal finances. As I mentioned at the start of this chapter, some people naively wish to jump past the first three steps and find some investment that will pay them handsomely. Rather than working, managing their money and accruing savings, they seek funds for an investment scheme. I won't deny the possibility that such a plan could succeed. Occasionally people have remarkable success from unlikely or risky financial strategies, but the investing step is best applied as a fourth and final step in a solid personal-finances game plan.

Most financially successful people in the world are not just big investors. And I would even venture to say that most are not big risk-takers at all. Most are the turtles, not the rabbits. I think again of the dry-cleaning businesses that, at one time, had created more millionaires than any other type of business. The prudent, careful investor might not end up among the *richest* people in the world. Wildly wealthy people are generally those with family money, extraordinary luck, or unusual circumstances. On the other hand, the vast majority of financially successful people simply play by the basic rules. Referring back to the definition of financial success as having sufficient money to live well and be secure in your future, these people, in general, work hard, manage their money, save ably, and then invest—prudently. They're neither boring nor particularly afraid to take chances; they're simply wise when they invest. And they never risk everything.

Epilogue: Planning

By failing to prepare, you are preparing to fail.
-Benjamin Franklin

Have a Plan

Financial planning—having a financial plan for your working life and retirement—is an epilogue to the four rules. I understand that planning for your financial future is not for everyone. Some people prefer being serendipitous and whimsical in all areas of their life. If I'm honest, I must admit that some of those serendipitous people lead charmed lives that always seem to turn out well. On the other hand, I can also safely say that I know some very nice people who have lived happily, but fancifully, and ended up in austere circumstances in their waning years.

I advocate for you to have a plan. There are many simple online apps and calculators to help you. I found this list of good planning tools online:

- Fidelity's myPlan Snapshot
- Personal Capital's Retirement Planner
- Betterment's Retirement Savings Calculator
- Stash's Retirement Calculator
- Charles Schwab's Retirement Savings Calculator
- Vanguard's Retirement Nest Egg Calculator

Just plug in your numbers. Many such planners guide you through the entire process. If you have an account at the institution, a 401(k) or an IRA, at Fidelity, Charles Schwab or Vanguard, for example, the planners are available to you for no extra cost. I particularly like Fidelity's planning tools. You can adjust your saving strategies to see how you will fare long-term. As I mentioned, some people find such bold-faced clarity about their finances too engineered, but if you've read this book up to this point, I suspect you have at least some interest in financial security. Having a plan and using planning tools make you much more likely to execute at least an approximation of that plan. Like the old saying goes, *"If you don't look where you're going, you might not like where you end up."*

If you really find that planning has too many moving parts, you can seek professional advice. As mentioned, you should be cautious of accepting financial planning advice from those employed by or allied with investment institutions, or, even more dangerously, with specific investments. Opt for an independent, fee-based financial planner, if at all possible. Or utilize planning assistance offered through not-for-profit agencies such as AARP (American Association of Retired Persons), which are more likely to be free from specific institutional or product influences.

No Grand Plan Required

I don't want to imply that you must have some detailed or elaborate plan. You may have a loose or very simple plan. Knowing your current overhead, you can easily estimate the monthly budget you'll need to cover your basic expenses and maintain a similar lifestyle in retirement. Then compare that amount to the income resources you'll have—income from social security, income from a pension, if you will have one, and income from monthly disbursements from your savings. If the budget looks good for 30 years or so, you can feel relatively confident.

If it seems clear that your savings will probably not last for the number of years you are likely to live, one of the simplest adjustments you can make is to continue working for a few more years to save more and reduce the number of years you will need to fund with savings dollars. Or, you can plan to reduce your overhead, for example by moving to a smaller home or to a less expensive area. Or, you can consider a "phase two" plan for later retirement years, involving reductions or moves sometime in the future.

Maybe you are in that population that aspires to retire by 50, 55 or 60. Understand when you plan for such an early retirement age that with today's life expectancies you are looking at a *very* long retirement. From age 50 you are likely to live an additional *40-45 years*. That is a very long period of time to sponsor financially without active income. Even if you are in a job that will offer a nice pension, if you hope to retire comfortably make sure to run numbers. Then, even if your numbers look acceptable, you should think through various contingency or conservation plans. Frankly even at traditional retirement age, which is 65ish, 30 years is a long haul and should involve prudent Plan Bs.

On the flip side of the early retirement planners, are those that think they will "never retire." Such a plan is admirable and certainly more viable than in past history when mandatory retirement or agism might have pushed you out of active employment. Older people are generally healthier today and may laws protect them from the most overt kinds of age discrimination. But if this is your plan, be aware that your intention is fine but what actually comes to pass may not be subject to choice.

Conservation Plans & Plan Bs

As with careers, not every retirement strategy goes according to plan. The economy could take a dramatic turn. You could have a serious health challenge. Ask yourself what you might do if life throws your retirement plans for a loop. The answer is not to continue blindly with the plan, hoping that life will somehow miraculously put your finances back on track. At least consider what your fallback position, your Plan B, would be.

Is there a possible conservation strategy you might utilize? What expenses might you eliminate if you needed to? Might you invite a trusted friend or relative to live with you and share expenses? Or you with them while you rent out your home for some time to recoup deficit dollars? One woman I know airbnb'd her family home for just one year and was able to collect a remarkable stash of retirement dollars. Might you consider selling your home or other key valuables? Might you find some part-time work you could enjoy, possibly doing consulting or support work for your former employer or utilizing one of your back-pocket skills?

I reflect again on the case study of the couple who launched a new business just before the pandemic hit. Forced to shut down for months, this couple consumed all their available savings and retirement dollars. When life throws your plans for a loop, as life sometimes does, if you have a Plan B, you can more successfully navigate and ride out the unexpected challenge. You may not *want* to deploy a conservation plan, but the alternative is to allow the unexpected to put your future at risk. When in retirement, or close to it, without a strategy you may be incapable of reversing the damage.

Simple Case Studies
Here are a few case studies of some real, average people I know in as they approached or entered retirement.

— *Alex*

The first case study involves a friend, whom I will call Alex, who was never particularly financially attentive, other than to consistently work and zealously safeguard her credit. Her approach to life was to live modestly but comfortably, forgoing any debt other than a car and very short-term purchase debt, such as for a new appliance or a vacation, which would be paid off in a matter of months. Alex worked for the state government for over 25 years, starting in an entry-level position, then being promoted to progressively more senior roles. For the last ten years or so of her employment, she contributed to a deferred-compensation savings program she was offered. But Alex contributed no more than a couple hundred dollars per month, and being quite risk-averse, she invested those dollars only in the money-market option, essentially just a savings account, so that her savings growth was never substantial. Alex drew her financial security from a known, vested pension that she was eligible for upon retirement.

When Alex did retire and began to collect her pension, she happily found her lifestyle changed little. She had always lived frugally, and her pension "take-home" very nearly equaled her working years paycheck once all job deductions and costs were accounted for. Now, as a retired person, Alex picks up occasional work hours at a local school and rarely taps any of her modest savings. Since she is comfortable, she is holding off on collecting social security, for which she is also eligible, at a much-reduced level due to her government pension. But those dollars will help Alex in later years when she might not be able to pick up the occasional days of work.

Alex's comfortable situation comes primarily from her choices involving the first rule, work. She was willing to start at the entry level in a secure job. That job also offered the invaluable, and relatively rare, perk of a pension. She was diligent about working and advanced in her career numerous times. This improved Alex's income while she was working and boosted her later pension amount. Alex wasn't particularly attentive to the other rules. She didn't do much managing of her financial budget, other than being savvy enough to avoid overspending and dangerous debt. Alex only utilized passive savings in modest amounts. She did no investing. Still, in the end, Alex is a personal-finance success story. In this case, the work choice was key, and it shows that work really can be a pivotal factor in personal-finance success.

— *Joe*

Now let's consider another friend's story. Joe was also a diligent, long-term employee, in this case for a large corporation. He advanced to be a mid-level manager and stayed with his company for over thirty years. Joe was married and had two children, though he and his wife divorced soon after the kids reached adulthood. Throughout his career, Joe saved and invested using the 401(k) at his corporation, but twice tapped those funds for personal expenses—once to cover a period of his wife's unemployment, and once to pay for one of his kids' education. At about fifty years of age, after the divorce, and once both of his kids were self-supporting, Joe began rebuilding his retirement savings in earnest. The investment options he selected in his 401(k) were based on the institution's recommendation and were fairly conservative due to his age.

I sat with Joe when he was in his early sixties, and we plugged his numbers into a retirement calculator. He hoped to retire within the next year or two, but he was not encouraged by what the calculator projected. He had collected over $300K in his replenished retirement account and knew how much social security he would have, assuming he deferred collecting until full retirement age. Between the two, and projecting a 30-year retirement, he would be unable to maintain his condo mortgage payment and association fees when combined with his other living expenses. The mortgage was newer, refinanced just recently, so it would be in play for most of his retirement years. He tried eliminating a car payment, saying, "I'll just keep this car forever." He also tried to eliminate any entertainment or vacation allowance, saying, "I'll stay home." He even tried a 20-year retirement scenario, gamely suggesting that he could off himself if he appeared likely to live beyond age 80. In the end, I suggested he ramp up his savings to the maximum and consider working just a few more years, in order to shorten the financial gap between leaving his job and full social security. Joe was sullen when we finished up.

After thirty years of hard work, Joe was naturally disappointed that he wasn't in a position to easily retire. How did that happen? Clearly, Joe had embraced the work rule. He also managed his finances and overhead with a busy home and family. He successfully raised two productive kids. Though Joe gave some consideration to saving and investing, even early in his work career, he did not consider those funds sacrosanct. If he had resisted the pressure to tap his retirement savings twice, his retirement story would likely be somewhat different. In chatting with Joe about this, he became more sanguine. He loved his kids and had enjoyed good times with his wife and family in their years together. He didn't want to regret any of it. With that realization, Joe embraced the last leg of his work career, and as of this writing is living frugally to pound out some savings so he can be better positioned for retirement when it comes.

— *Christina*

This next story is different. Christina worked in sales. During her career, she moved around to many different companies, spending a few years here and a few years there. When times were good, Christina made excellent money, often in the six figures. While employed, Christina participated in workplace 401(k)s, but she cashed out the funds for interim living money whenever she left a job. When her mother passed away, Christina inherited a senior-living condo that was paid off, a one-time boon from her humble family. So, in her mid-fifties, Christina moved from the West to East Coast to take up residence in the condo. At that time, Christina wanted to continue working but struggled to find a good job. Finally, she ended up accepting a lower-level job with an online retailer, and she plans to eke out the next few years until she is eligible for her social security benefits. She has little savings.

Christina's situation isn't uncommon. Many people have little money saved and in retirement will be seeking a living situation where they can survive on the modest social security benefit they will eventually receive. Christina is lucky to have a quite comfortable, low-cost place to live. Others end up in a spare room of a family member or in other diminished settings. Christina will not be traveling or enjoying fancy living, but she can maintain a modest, independent life.

— Sue

Lest you think that changing jobs regularly equates to financial insecurity, let's look at another scenario—mine. As I shared earlier, I didn't really begin to be particularly financially responsible until my thirties. Before that time, I worked consistently, but always in marginal, extremely low-paying jobs. I kept myself afloat, but just. In my early thirties, I went to work for a corporation and stayed long enough to start making what was for me a more substantial salary, although it was relatively modest compared to what others might consider real money. Given my new financial circumstances, and having no prior experience or understanding of money management, I began, as I shared in other sections, studying various money-management books on my own.

During that time, I made two good decisions. I started utilizing the 401(k)-retirement plan at work, and I bought a house. I worked at that particular corporation for about six years, and then I moved to another corporation for a year, followed by another for two years, and then to another for another two more years. The moves were sometimes by my choice or sometimes due to corporate restructuring, but two things never changed. One, I was respectful to the companies as I departed and aggressive about getting into a next job. And two, I contributed money to the 401(k)s at each company and, despite the financial constraints that came during transitions, I never tapped any of those retirement accounts. The house, bought when the housing market was at a low, was a great purchase and is a sizable source of equity for me some 20+ years later. But I cannot take much credit for that profitable outcome. On the other hand, I do take some pride in my savings. Transition times were a challenge, and in addition I had several lean years between leaving my last cushy corporate role in the mid-2000s and launching a consulting business. Still, I did not touch those savings. When things got tough, I sold my gold, liquidated all the individual stocks I owned, and refinanced my house to lower the payment. I even considered night jobs or a return to corporate employment, but thankfully did not need to take those measures. Through all the lean times, though, I never touched the retirement money.

As my financial circumstances improved after the recession, I recommenced saving for retirement and eventually did decide to return to corporate employment. To supplement my renewed 401(k) savings, I reestablished a new, small-stock portfolio, added some deferred comp, and funneled some after-tax dollars to CD savings. When I plug *my* numbers into the retirement planning calculator, I am rewarded with a green light for my retirement plan.

I must admit that at least part of the comfort I feel about my upcoming retirement comes from my spouse's financial contributions. Together, our projected retirement numbers look quite comfortable. That said, I also do calculations for other "what if" contingencies. Though things look rosy right now, we know that a significant blip could occur, and our circumstances could change. Our Plan B is to rent out our little back house/office if needed, or even to move into the office ourselves and rent out our main house. The worst-case contingency scenario would be to sell off our house, which has, happily, considerable equity available.

I use my own example because I don't want to imply that the only path to financial security is through a long career in one company or organization. You can make career transitions, as I have certainly done. You can strike out on your own. You can go through a rough patch. In doing so, you *can* keep an overall financial plan in mind. Going all-in on some endeavor may sound daring and romantic, but people who gamble in this way sometimes do lose it all. Eating up your retirement savings because you cannot find a suitable or desirable job, or your business is struggling, is a possible option, but may have significant long-term ramifications. Find *any* job, understanding it may be temporary, or dramatically tighten your belt instead. Sell some of your belongings. Retrench your living situation. Through every transition and current career gambit, you need to remember that you are committed to a bigger plan and are not just hoping for things to turn out well or turn around. You're in charge of keeping your financial future secure.

— *Jon*

The last case I want to discuss is of an entrepreneur/ small business owner. As I mentioned, I was self-employed for about ten years, but the case I will highlight is of another small business owner, Jon. Jon had no interest in school or traditional business as a young man. As a teen Jon dabbled in criminal activities but was fortunate enough to be hired in his early twenties by a pool company to work in the field cleaning pools. He liked it very much. So much so that within a few years, he hung a shingle, gathered his first few pool customers, and went into the business. He grew that business over the years, and, once established, made an excellent income for over 30 years. He bought a nice house, raised two kids, had great cars, took regular vacations, and played lots of golf.

At sixty-two, however, Jon had a stroke. He had health insurance, so there was no particular financial impact from the medical bills but once the initial crisis passed, Jon was told his recovery would be a long one. Jon's income continued as his workers kept doing their jobs, but without active oversight, Jon knew quality issues and poaching could erode the value of his business. He considered selling but knew he would not be selling from a position of strength, and he would be lucky to get anywhere close to his business's book value.

This difficult financial situation is still playing out for Jon and his wife, who also works. Jon demonstrated that the self-employed *can* make good, even excellent, money. One of the biggest challenges for the self-employed, however, is to be disciplined in preparing and planning for contingencies and retirement. Jon believed that retirement was still many years off. He had only a loose plan to sell off his business at some point and use the sale dollars as his nest egg. That plan is now at risk. Fortunately, Jon had paid off his house early on and owned most of his vehicles. Though he had some savings, he and his wife will now face a significantly altered retirement picture. If you choose a self-employment option, make sure you take advantage of some of the great retirement saving options available for small businesses mentioned in the last section.

Health Insurance

Speaking of health challenges, let me stress the need for health insurance coverage in whatever financial and retirement plans you have. On some level we know that serious illness can wipe out even the most robust financial plans. Obtaining and maintaining health care coverage is one of the primary protections you can give your financial future. Lapses in health care coverage can expose you and your family to dreaded pre-existing-conditions exclusions, so don't think that foregoing this coverage because you are young or relatively healthy is prudent. If you *are* young and healthy, opt for the lowest cost/ highest-deductible coverage you can find, but don't play the dangerous game of going without insurance. Again, without insurance, even a common car accident or slip in the driveway can lead to a serious depletion of your hard-saved resources. As a country, we are still deciding if health coverage will be required by law, but as a financial-prudence measure, having this protection is worth every penny, as health-related injury or illness have historically been a leading cause of many people's financial ruin. Even if you are or become unemployed, new laws currently mandate that you be offered a sliding-scale payment for your health insurance program. Protect yourself in this way, and few other threats are as likely to take you down financially.

Of course, at age 65, you will become eligible for Medicare, parts of which are free, and parts of which are nominally priced. Medicare is a real blessing for our senior population. Still, Medicare provides only limited healthcare coverage, and you are encouraged to consider Medigap or some other form of "gap" healthcare insurance to supplement the standard Medicare coverage. In planning for Medicare gap coverage, be aware of the six-month open enrollment window, when you may not be denied a policy or coverage because of your health status. This window is only offered once, when you are approaching age 65, and is strictly managed. Regardless of other healthcare plans or coverage you might have—if for example, you're still working—you should nevertheless address the Medicare and gap-insurance application process as Medicare prescribes during this crucial window of time.

Long Term Care (LTC) Insurance

Having this coverage could save your finances in your waning years but make no mistake: it's expensive. If you or your spouse have a family history of lingering and ultimately debilitating illnesses, such as strokes, Alzheimer's, MS, Parkinson's, diabetes, kidney failure, or liver issues, just to name a few, you might want to add this type of insurance to your retirement planning. Even if the plan covers only a portion of the cost of the LTC, it can save an older individual or couple from devasting but necessary costs. Typical healthcare insurance and Medicare cover only a limited number of days of this type of care. Many illnesses and injuries will require significantly more days, often months or years of care. Without LTC insurance, you might be faced with the decision to pay for the care out of pocket, or to forego the care altogether. Not good options.

I always thought that I would, if faced with such debilitation, choose to forego treatment and take my chances.

But as I advance in age, I instead find myself preferring the option of accepting treatments. Also, I'm married to someone who expects that we will get all the care that's recommended. Build in the cost of LTC into your plan and apply early. Upon retirement, try to lock in your rate. Rates for premiums go up dramatically as you age, and coverage is lowest when you haven't already been diagnosed with a debilitating disorder. So, again, investigate your options and apply early.

Life Insurance

Humm, life insurance. A life insurance plan while you're working is usually reasonably priced, particularly if sponsored by an employer, and is crucial if you have a family and want to be sure that your loved ones will be able to carry on financially if something happens to you. In fact I recommend *anyone of working age with underage children* purchase some amount of life insurance, preferably an amount equaling two or more years of your income to protect against the unimaginable and to provide a life transition cushion. But beware the life-insurance salesman, presenting insurance as an investment. Bah! And, once your kids are grown, life insurance has little to commend it, other than a nefarious incentive for a tragic family homicide. Okay, maybe I watch too many true-crime shows. But seriously, protect your family with life insurance only while they require your support. Otherwise, there are better uses for your money.

Annuities

As pensions have become less common, annuities are being pushed by some financial planners. An annuity is a lifetime income, like a pension, that you purchase. But beware. If you have enough retirement savings to purchase an annuity, you probably have enough to simply disburse a similar monthly amount from your savings. No annuity required. They sell you on the annuity by promising you'll receive the money no matter how long you live, making you fearful that you will outlive your savings. But that lump of money that you hand over today for the annuity could and likely would grow, possibly significantly, while in the 401(k) or retirement account. The annuity is a fixed amount that has no potential for growth other than a possible, occasional cost-of-living adjustment. And while some annuities may offer a residual to an heir, which diminishes and ends over time, make no mistake: an annuity is a product offered by a *for-profit* company. Annuities are structured to make, never to lose, money for the company.

Reverse Mortgages

If you bought a home along the way and have substantial equity, retirement is the usual time to cash out on that wealth. Still, many retirees do not want to leave their home just to reap the profits. What can they do? One option is to take out a reverse mortgage. Reverse mortgages are available to persons in their sixties or older if they have considerable equity in their home or own it outright. The new "reverse" mortgage pays you either a lump sum disbursement or smaller monthly distributions, but in either case you can continue living in the home, mortgage-free, indefinitely (though you will still need to maintain home insurance and pay property tax). There are restrictions and stipulations, of course, and fees and interest charges are these loans are relatively high. In the coming years, I suspect the terms for reverse mortgages will improve, as they've already done somewhat over recent years, but even in today's form a reverse mortgage may make sense for some retirees.

Women and Finances

Women should read this section carefully. Men can read it less thoughtfully, although most men will have family members—a mother, a daughter, or even their own wife—for whom this section might apply. It's well known that women make less money than men, even for the same job—currently about 85 cents for every dollar a man makes. To increase the financial risk, women are also much less likely to save, and when they do save, they're less ambitious about it. Men, when polled, have an average savings goal for retirement of $400,000, versus the goal of only $200,000 that women typically average. Furthermore, only 57% of women are consistently employed full-time, additionally inhibiting their ability to save. Cultural and gender role stereotypes, and, of course, motherhood, are often factors in women not being employed or fully employed during their peak career-growth years. But even when working, only 45% of women participate in their workplace retirement-savings plans.

Despite this lesser focus on financial planning and security, between 80 and 90% of women will at some point be financially responsible for themselves, whether through death, divorce, or disability. And, of course, women have a longer life expectancy of 81 years, which is almost ten years beyond men's 73 years. By age 40, two-thirds of women have already dealt with a major financial crisis such as job loss—their own or their spouse's—divorce, death, or their own or their spouse's serious illness. Every year over age 40, the chances of experiencing some kind of financial misfortune grows. By age 50, almost 25% of women are *already* living alone, versus 12% of men. The average age of widowhood is 55, and a woman is three times more likely to be widowed than a man.

Furthermore, the largest category of growth in divorce rates is for couples over 50, the rate having doubled since 1990. In America, single women are the *poorest* group of older Americans, making up 75% of the elderly poor. It's also worth mentioning that 80% of poor elderly women were not poor prior to the death of their spouse or their divorce. The number of middle and upper-middle-class women who are struggling with debt or money issues in retirement is rising precipitously, and only a paltry 20% of women feel "confident" in their ability to manage their own finances in retirement. Many will depend on family members or acquaintances to help them manage their finances, putting them at risk for abuses, scams, and potential mismanagement issues.

Learning about personal finances and how to competently manage money is critical for all our young people, but it's a crisis-level issue for women. I recommend to all women reading this book, or parents of girls, to spend time becoming financially aware. What exactly do I mean by that? Here are a few suggestions.

If you're married, sit with your spouse and a notepad, and learn the details of your household finances. How much is coming in and how much is going out? Where are your savings and how much do you have? Are you investing? Exactly how much and where are the investments? You might ask to take over managing the finances for your household either for a short time or permanently. Earlier in this chapter I described the case study of Jon who had a stroke. Jon's wife, Jamie, had a very rude awakening and a very immediate need to learn the details of the household finances. Jon was unconscious and not able to answer any questions or assist her in any way. He had taken care of all the bills, but while he was in the hospital for months, Jamie had to figure out what needed to be paid and how. I remember her sharing her horror at the amount of their household electric bill. She suddenly found herself caring about her son's tendency to crank up the AC every afternoon. In some ways Jamie was lucky. She was forced to learn and become capable of managing the family finances, and she still was blessed with having her husband come home from the hospital to continue sharing her life. Many other women are not so lucky.

If you do not know already, then ask about your spouse's career and retirement game plan. Ask how they see your retirement years playing out. I'm so disheartened at how many women feel they aren't entitled to or capable of knowing about their communal finances. It's your life too! Together, create or review your retirement budget and determine if the current plan is viable. It's better to know early on that you only have saved enough to cover your existing monthly overhead for 5, 10, or 15 years. Well, guess what, you are *both* very likely to live 20 or even 30 years in retirement! What's the plan for the remaining years? What is the "phase two" plan for when the money runs out? Can you economize early in retirement to make your dollars last longer? Will re-trenching be required?

What provisions are in place for you, in particular? What will happen to you if your spouse dies or becomes infirm? If your spouse has a pension that your current finances depend on, will the pension continue for you if your spouse passes away? You need to know these answers. Remember, statistically speaking, you're *likely* to have to take over and manage your finances on your own at some point. It's more likely than not. Educate yourself.

If your spouse is uncooperative, well, that's tricky. Maybe they feel the money is "theirs." Perhaps they are embarrassed to share the reality of your finances. Or they might see such questions as a challenge to their financial prowess. Try to learn what you can on your own and keep asking for information. Having a spouse who doesn't want to share details of your joint finances doesn't necessarily mean that you're in trouble, but I still recommend you have a Plan B.

Plan B? Really? Yes, really. As a couple, what might you do if serious financial challenges arise? At least give it some thought. Or, and this is hard, what might you do if you were left on your own? This may not be down to a shoddy spouse or desertion but could easily happen based on an unfortunate turn of events, illness, or death. Are you prepared for such a turn?

If you're currently working, whether you provide your household's primary or secondary income, stop considering your work unimportant. Reread the section on working. Choose to step up and embrace the work that you do. If you find it hard to do that, think about a transition. Your age doesn't matter. Ask yourself, is there something you've always wanted to do? Is there some career out there for you to aspire to? Choose to be ambitious career-wise. Thinking that your income doesn't matter is part of a common learned helplessness that exists in too many women. Choose to be ambitious and make money.

Then, make yourself a personal budget, manage your income, and create your own savings goals. Disentangle your personal finances from joint finances if you're married. Not as a rebellion, but as practice. Try to integrate strong financial management on your own. In particular, treat your income as money that needs to be managed, not as some kind of supplemental or play money. The day may come when that money and money-management skill will be critical for you. Take your income seriously, even if your spouse or family pays all your bills, and even if you're sure that you won't need to worry about money later in life. Better to be capable of managing and not need to, than to need to and not know how, especially as you get older.

Legacy Funds, Bequests, and Wills

Rich people always leave behind big dollars for their heirs. They have so much money and so many assets that inevitably there will be an inheritance. But even modestly successful people may have some dollars and assets to leave to their kids or other heirs. As already mentioned, I've never received any such funds, though both my parents and assorted other relatives have passed on. On the other hand, my spouse, though not from a wealthy family, did receive nice bequests from her mother and other elders in her family who passed away.

If you suppose that you will have money or assets to pass on, you will need a will to delineate your preferences. A living trust, where you essentially transfer property or assets in advance, can greatly facilitate eventually bequeathing property to your heirs. It's frequently put in place while creating your will. Both wills and living trusts are fairly simple and inexpensive to create. You just need to decide who will inherit and how much, which is often expressed as a percentage, as the final dollar amount available may be unknown. If you're married, creating a will must be done collaboratively with your spouse. Your spouse is, of course, in most cases, the first-level beneficiary of your money and assets. But if you want to ensure money or assets are passed to others, for example your kids from a previous marriage, which is a common scenario, you need to formally draft the instructions with your spouse's consent and understanding.

You should also consider drafting a so-called "living will" or advanced directive to establish your preferences for medical care if you become incapacitated by injury or illness. Rather than place the burden of decision-making on your spouse or other family members, such instructions about life-support, heroic life-saving measures, or resuscitation can provide your family with comfort and clarity about your wishes in what might be terribly trying times.

Final Words

I began writing this book as a primer for friends and family on how to achieve financial security from the perspective of an average person who has never been given helpful guidance in personal finances. It started with a single sheet of paper I titled "Wise Up about Finances" with short explanations of the four rules. Over the years, I shared that simple set of rules with family members and some of the young people in my circle of friends. I like to think it made an impact and helped them with decision-making. The fact that many of these young people, and others that were not so young, sought further guidance from me says that something about the four rules did resonate with them.

This book, which expands on the concepts from that single sheet of paper, is intended to create actionable steps and an expanded perspective on each of the financial rules. Generally, personal finance is not rocket science. Anyone can do it. It starts with just getting a job and making money. Nothing extraordinary, just get a job. In my role as a consultant and doing corporate training and career development, I've counseled many people on career issues. I'm also involved with recovery programs that provide abundant examples and cases of life transformations based on simple steps taken one at a time.

Still, all career improvements start with actually working. That is, and always must be, the starting place. Managing and wealth-building cannot begin until the first rule is attended to. Careers are long, and advancement and better income are achievable for those willing to work, work hard, and in some cases thoughtfully transition.

As I approach my own retirement from corporate life, my goal in writing this book is to offer back some of the practical advice I found through experience, sometimes hard experience, and through personal research and ultimately good fortune. I encourage parents, teachers, and counselors to share this book with their kids, their students, their families or their clients to give hope and real-world guidance on personal finances. I also hope it can be a self-help guide for young people and not-so-young people who are struggling with their finances and might benefit from these simple lessons. That's the "wise-up" part of this message.

Furthermore, I believe that despite wide-ranging media and resources available, our current society does little to specifically educate average-to-lower-income Americans financially or support good financial practices. There are many traps in money management—credit traps, image traps, and the like. I fell into some of those traps myself and spent years living a financially marginal life. Those traps particularly impact low- to mid-income people and can create chronic financial problems.

I don't believe our government, or any government for that matter, can alleviate all its citizens' financial challenges. At best, government might offer scanty subsistence measures for the financially challenged. But *you* can learn to do better. You can learn about, overcome, and avoid the common traps in managing finances and thereby avoid all-too-common financial woes prevalent among today's average workers. That's the "rise up" part of this message.

Becoming financially responsible and eventually financially secure is up to you. It's in your power and is actually pretty simple, though admittedly not easy. You just have to choose to make the changes. It's never too late to embrace and take personal responsibility for yourself and your future.

I want to thank all the many people in my life who helped make this book possible, including my spouse, family, and many friends. I also want to thank all the various employers I've had over the years for their financial contributions to my life and experience. Finally, I want to particularly thank those whose personal stories I used. In most cases I changed names and some of the more specific features, but all of the case studies and stories are real, and I believe significantly enhanced the authenticity and value of the book's advice.

Made in the USA
Monee, IL
17 July 2022